WILLIS M. TATE
Views and Interviews

WILLIS M. TATE
Views
and
Interviews

Edited by Johnnie Marie Grimes

Introduction by Marshall Terry

SMU PRESS • DALLAS

© 1978 • SOUTHERN METHODIST UNIVERSITY PRESS • DALLAS

Library of Congress Cataloging in Publication Data
Tate, Willis M.
    Willis M. Tate : views and interviews.

    1. Education, Higher—United States—Aims and objectives—Ad-
dresses, essays, lectures. I. Grimes, Johnnie Marie, 1905-
LB2325.T29   378.73   77-25103
ISBN 0-87074-163-2

To the memory of

EUGENE McELVANEY

As a member of the
Southern Methodist University Board of Trustees (1939-71),
chairman of the board from 1960 to 1971, and
chairman of its executive committee from 1950 to 1964,
he brought a new depth to the role of trustee,
exemplifying during a period of great change
in higher education
the nature of true partnership
between a responsible trustee
and the chief executive officer of the university

Progress has always come when current presuppositions have been held in constant self-criticism. Liberties and privileges we enjoy today have come from this spirit of believing and questioning, at the same time knowing that truth is its own defense and the reward for the conscientious searcher.

Only when a nation is dedicated to freedom can such an institution as this endure. Just as surely a nation remains free only as universities are free in their quest for truth.

Here, then, is our challenge and our commitment: to create and maintain an atmosphere of friendly cooperation, a fellowship of growing personalities, an environment of inquiry, a colony of democratic living, and a scene for adventures of the spirit.

—WILLIS M. TATE, responding
at his inauguration
May 5, 1955

Contents

PART TWO

INTERVIEWS

Illustrations are grouped following page 70

Preface

DURING THE EIGHTEEN YEARS of Willis McDonald Tate's presidency of Southern Methodist University (1954-1972), institutions of higher learning moved through several periods when the nature of higher education and the role of the college and university were questioned. They were praised, attacked, manipulated, drowned in grants, and finally left to a normalcy that can best be described as austerity.

The population explosion began to be felt. The launching of the space ape dramatically affected higher education. The floodgates opened for federal funding, especially in science and technology, providing both opportunity and peril to a university's understanding of its purpose. Liberal learning was perennially predicted to be at worst obsolete, or at best in need of reform, at a time when undergraduates were urgently searching for personal and social cohesion. Institutions of higher learning dramatically increased in number; colleges and universities in state systems doubled. In America's dual system of higher education, public and private institutions struggled for clarity and identity and competed for their share of the tax and philanthropic dollar.

In the midst of a decade of growth and unprecedented public support, colleges and universities saw the young rise up to question the leadership of their elders. They cried for change, and at times they rejected the institutional forms and educational content available to them. The temptation to allow itself to be uncritically used or manipulated by larger forces in society severely tested a university's own understanding of its mission. A president of any university, and especially a major university, needed to be very clear about his institution's purpose.

It was not without cause, therefore, that President Tate acknowledged many times that his major concern was to interpret the nature of higher education in general and of Southern Methodist University in particular. These interpretations were made to the SMU community and to its various publics in private conversations, in board and committee meetings, in budget hearings, in discussions with students and faculty, and in official public statements and writings.

A statement or essay presented here as reflecting President Tate's views deals with an issue which was alive at the time it was expressed. It was relevant to the character of Southern Methodist University. It also is alive today. The past stands beside the present, helping to find new answers from old experiences. In most instances, a statement or an essay dealt with an issue the understanding of which led President Tate to act in a certain way or was an interpretation of action taken or not taken. In other instances the views expressed were a part of the president's own developing rationale as he led SMU through dynamic and changing years.

The selections range in time from 1954 to 1972. They were prepared for a wide range of primary audiences. Transcending these differences, however, is a common bond; the concern of the president to interpret the purpose of a university in general and Southern Methodist University in particular.

A brief description of the context within which each view was expressed is included.

I have known President Tate for over thirty years, and have worked with him at Southern Methodist University for twenty-two years. I have been close to the seat of power and have seen the president function in a great variety of situations. This collection of his views and the context within which he expressed them is designed to give some insight into the trauma, the delights, the ambiguities of the office of the president of Southern Methodist University during a particular period of time, as I observed it at close range. I have sought President Tate's counsel and his remembrances, but he neither expected nor used any veto power over anything in this book. I am in no way to be thought of as objective. An objective, critical history of Southern Methodist University from 1954 to 1972 will be written by someone, some day. Perhaps this collection of "views and interviews" may be useful as one source.

For their assistance in the editing of this volume, my warmest thanks go to my husband, Professor Howard Grimes, for encouragement and real support (he was patient when I interrupted his own work, and he cooked many meals while I struggled to find lost footnotes and resolve conflicting sources); to Professor Marshall Terry for his willingness to contribute a perceptive introduction; to Decherd Turner, librarian of Bridwell Library, for the generous loan of a carrel; to Marian Cleary, President Tate's administrative assistant, for her tireless efforts in pursuing details; to Phoebe Davis, Frank Seay, Gerald McGee, Kate Warnick, the staff of the SMU Archives, and the librarians of all SMU libraries for various forms of assistance; to Allen Maxwell and Margaret Hartley of the SMU Press and former Vice President Larry Ter Molen for helpful advice at significant moments; and finally, to President Tate for trusting me to offer this interpretation of his presidency of Southern Methodist University.

JOHNNIE MARIE GRIMES
Dallas, Texas
January, 1978

Introduction

Willis Tate: A Recollection of Character

THIS IS NOT MY BOOK about Willis Tate, whose whole life and career have been Southern Methodist University and whose leadership of the university spanned more than twenty years, but a brief introduction to a selection of his speeches—speeches whose subjects were important at the time and whose themes were always characteristic of the ideas, beliefs, and styles of the man who became the "living visible symbol" of the university.

I write from the perspective, first, of a young person dedicated to the university and to Willis Tate's own beliefs, one who served for eight years in Tate's administration doing mostly the interpretive work he considered so vital; then, from the perspective of an older person, a faculty member whose dedication to the idea of a free private university—one of so few in the American Southwest—has been always equal to my interest in my own particular discipline and department.

And I must also write from the perspective of one who has steadily cherished, no matter what disagreement there may have been on specific issues along the way, the personal and professional association with Willis Tate, whose qualities of loyalty to institution and to human beings, whose integrity, hard and endless work for the good cause, and social and educational statesmanship I much admire.

Nothing is clearer to me now than that Tate, that most pragmatic man, inspired personal devotion and devotion to an idea and ideal of the university we believed must emerge here. He inspired this devotion in myself and in others, and it holds. It is also clear that Tate's own devotion and his immense "staying power" came from his church background and

xvii

his deep personal religious faith. He was able, as are few people I have known, to embrace steadily the whole of his situation, and in times of adversity to keep calmly to the course he believed in, because, I think, he had a sense not only of thought-out purpose but of his faith, of God's grace.

The accomplishments of Willis Tate's presidency are recorded elsewhere, though there is a volume to be written dealing fully with the Tate years, when the time is ripe. Tate's time encompassed the problems in the nation, the level of higher educational aims and realities in our region, and the peculiar possibilities of the attitudes toward university education in Dallas during the crucial last five years of the 50s, the burgeoning demands of the 60s, and the strange conditions of the early 70s. These were not easy times to be an educational leader, and Tate's tenure as president is remarkable for its record-setting length, for its success in turning SMU from a small Texas school into what our chaplain once called "a sure enough university," and for the durability of Tate's aims and ideas.

Johnnie Marie Grimes, the wonderfully energetic and humane adviser who served Tate longest and most closely during these years, has organized this collection into sections reflecting the basic kinds of issues Tate concerned himself with on behalf of the university, the ideas, issues, and conditions he spoke to again and again through his term to his basic audiences of students, faculty, the Academy, the alumni, and SMU's environing and not always sympathetic publics. She has added some valuable interview material. She has provided a context for each speech. This is helpful, for each talk needs to be understood as rooted in the circumstances of the occasion, of the time.

Tate was a superb speaker who believed his first responsibility as president was to interpret the university to those outside it, so it could go on with its true work. He had the art of addressing complex problems in simple, understandable terms, at the same time not oversimplifying or reducing the subject; the art of the good teacher. While least effective in speaking to his faculty—he had trouble understanding and relating to the critical faculty mind, felt more insecure in their presence than he ever should have because he had not quite finished his advanced degree, and tended to overgeneralize to them—he was marvelously clear and effective in speaking to businessmen, often in their own language, and to other public groups.

He would, for example, in his continuous process of educating the public that academic freedom was a *sine qua non* for a self-respecting university, use the terms "freedom of inquiry" or "the free marketplace of ideas." Let someone else use "*sine qua non*" or "academic freedom" on campus if he must; Tate knew his downtown audience might not understand, and so might resent, the one phrase and was fiercely suspicious of the other. So that when he spoke he was not making "self-evident" assertions for their own sake, he was educating. And often the audience would understand; and the situation would actually change because of that understanding.

Of course, Tate was a showman, too. Sometimes the faculty did not appreciate his going forth off campus to say what a circus he had to run back on the campus, so hold tight, folks, we're doing our almighty best. Nor appreciate such a speech as the classic and oft-delivered "The Care and Feeding of Professors." But when the occasion and seriousness of subject and the old, true clarity came together, Tate was terrific.

(You might begin by reading one of his first important talks, "What Is a University?" It is clear; it is beautifully simple; it is true; and it was, from the time it was first delivered, a central message.)

Inevitably, without the felt character and presence of the speaker, such speeches as those here assembled lose force, their purpose achieved. Their ideas, though bold when first advanced, may seem tame now because accepted. The situation of the moment is hard to imagine. All this may be truer of Tate's speeches than of those of others, for he brought another quality to his public statements that at times irritated me but which in retrospect I see as statesmanlike, certainly part of his basic method and makeup.

This was the quality of conciliation, of never being what he would have called "emotional" or "overdramatic" no matter how hot or tortured the issue or what villains opposed us: of being always on the highest plane and level of connotation that might reach people, in order not to antagonize but to persuade, to be *positive.* Looking over these speeches now, I see that the conviction was always there, sometimes courageously so; but he was more *qualified* than those public speakers whose dramatic utterances made headlines. I think he believed this qualification, this conciliation, to be two principles of the nature of life, qualification a principle of the nature of reality, conciliation of the nature of possibility. So that both principles operated as part of the conviction expressed. Tate was, by the same token, a man of long purpose, of real hopefulness, always eschewing the dart for the promise of the palm.

At any rate, the assembling of these speeches will be useful to future students of the man, the institution, or the times.

I remember, when Willis Tate was named president in 1954, I was a teaching fellow in English, sitting grading stacks of freshman themes in a basement office in Dallas Hall. A student came in to ask what I thought of the appointment of this new young president. There was some thought that he was not "academic" enough for the job. "Oh well," I remember saying, "how 'academic' do you have to be?" I did not know Tate then; a trustee had told me they selected him because he knew SMU, its hopes and problems and tradition, and because of his total dedication to the place. "The word is," I think I said, "he'll work like hell at it. And he sure *looks* like a president."

Now there is no doubt that all those things were true. The time was not right in Dallas, in my opinion, for a more high-pockets "academic" type or for an efficient manager type. What Tate had cut out for him to do was to establish the idea of SMU as potentially a "great university," after the gains made toward that end by the beloved Umphrey Lee. (How many years did we use the corny slogan "A Great City Deserves a Great University!" in the Sustentation campaign, and how deeply did we—and many in Dallas—believe it.) No, the person chosen to be the new president of SMU had to have Lee's warmth, the confidence of the church, and a more practical sense of scope, of the range of possibilities, than Lee had. The new leader had to be, at that stage, a generalist with the broadest possible appeal.

I think what Tate, in his early forties, vigorous youngest of the five presidents to that time, brought to his task was a double understanding of the SMU situation.

In the first place, he cherished, as all of us who choose to stay here come to cherish, SMU's founding tradition: that this institution, with a fine first faculty and student body, established by the church and by the citizens of Dallas on raw prairie with Jefferson's architecture, Yale and Harvard's colors, and an essential guiding motto, was meant to be from the beginning a first-rate university, nurtured in a religious faith but open to all viewpoints and not sectarian. In the second place, Tate brought an idea, instilled in him by this place which was his alma mater, of the nature of a university trying to develop beyond a simpler college. Somehow Tate always instinctively and deeply understood a *university's* dimensions of pursuing and giving learning, of service, and he understood those principles which must not be gainsaid and by which such progress might be measured.

This understanding he showed as he began his presidency by squarely facing the challenge of Professor John O. Beaty's anti-Semitism and attacks upon the SMU Press and *Southwest Review*. His strength and wisdom in this matter set the tone for his long administration.

As a novelist, and a rather old-fashioned one at that, again in tune with what I said to that student in 1954, I must comment on Tate's physical presence. He seemed, and was, a big man, handsome, interested in others, with an intense sense of the community that was the university. (Of "scholars mature and fledgling" in Albert Outler's phrase.) The confidence he inspired just simply physically and by his manner was significant: to students—he had come up dealing with students, and he always loved them as long as they did not aim to hurt the university; to the faculty, many of whom he defended quietly, without their ever knowing it, from attack because of their ideas; and to his trustees and to leaders in the local community, who might damn well dislike with all their liver and lights something that was going on at SMU but who would hold tight to their support of the place because of a deep personal regard and liking for Willis Tate.

As for working hard at it, there is a quotation from one of Emerson's essays which I think applies. (How Emersonian Tate suddenly appears, how moved by a universal faith and ethic, by self-reliance, by the work ethic of his Protestant forebears!)

"There is a time," the quotation goes, "in every man's education when he arrives at the conviction that envy is ignorance; that imitation is suicide; that he must take himself for better or for worse as his portion; that though the wide universe is full of good, no kernel of nourishing corn can come to him but through his toil bestowed on that plot of ground which is given him to till."

SMU was the soil Tate was given to till. He tilled it, I believe, night and day, waking and sleeping, until the university *was* his life almost completely.

He was, in this regard, never what my father used to call "a money player." Seventy percent was not good enough; he was a one hundred percenter in his efforts and his measurement of them. Many of his frustrations (and he was human enough to have frustrations and suffer them deeply, even at times to suffer a melancholia over them) came, I believe, from this attitude, when others in the university could not or would not share his absolute dedication and his perspectives on the university. There may have been a strain of the martyr in Tate, and sometimes I felt he found himself alone in the desert of his dream for SMU, wondering why others would not more absolutely help him crack the dry rock. Sometimes I think his gentleness was resignation, so that at the crucial times he would apply that principle of conciliation. Yet his quality of seeming larger than others came from the ability, or philosophy, of not abandoning hope, even when a deficit problem seemed insoluble or a cherished prospect lost.

Looking up the page at the Emerson quotation, I see the phrase "imitation is suicide" and begin to reflect on that. Tate never thought that we should take another university as a model for SMU. SMU was its own place in its own situation and should develop in its unique way. I ponder that, as we now begin to seek models—Yale, say, or Stanford—for our educational development. It always would have been easier to pick a certain model and try to re-create that here. In a way our educational philosophy may not have been strictly enough defined for optimum success (like a Ford grant) through the years. Perhaps our definition of a university, even *this* university, stayed too general and diffuse. I think what President Tate never clearly bridged—and what remains to be defined at SMU—was the two strains of its essential development.

One was the idea of a liberal arts oriented university whose every graduate would participate in a core curriculum of the humanities, social sciences, and sciences. The other was the idea of a university whose chief goal was "to serve society," especially through the establishment of strong professional schools. The Master Plan of 1963 affirmed the first, cohering idea, but also set in motion the development of one new and several existing but weak professional schools by strong "Lone Ranger" deans, going out on their own for their own interests. Well, while this was the central challenge and dilemma of Tate's last years, both ideas have "worked," you might say. For SMU retains a central humanistic philosophy that embraces in general-liberal courses all its students, while its professional schools have been greatly strengthened in recent years. And Tate's keeping to the broadest possible central definition was probably right. Certainly, as Mrs. Grimes remarks, his keeping to the concept of a "balanced" university in the time of the shriek for primarily technological development after Sputnik was courageous, unusual, and farsighted. (Two results of that: SMU still the "balanced" place; and its changeling child —Graduate Research Center, Inc. become Southwest Center for Advanced Studies become University of Texas at Dallas—sitting out north on *its* prairie. Both good results, I reckon.)

Because I realize that there was more to the man than his prose, that speeches turned documents invariably lose steam, I would like to reflect briefly on several incidents, during which I was close to Willis Tate. They happened at different times and may help bring a certain light, quite subjective, mind you, to the human side, the character, of Willis Tate.

In 1958 I returned to SMU, from writing advertising copy for another large Dallas phenomenon named Sam Bloom, to teach freshman English again and to assist Sterling Wheeler, then vice-president, in public relations for the university. Probably no university has had a tougher or more idealistic guardian of its basic values than Wheeler, in whose company facing the critics of SMU was a joyous battle. About the first thing that happened was that the *SMU Campus* announced that a student committee, on its own hook, had invited John Gates, avowed Communist and former editor of the *Daily Worker*, to speak on campus. These were Joe McCarthy times and, in Dallas, John Birch times of ultraconservatism when SMU already seemed scary pinko to many. In p.r. terms, Gates's visit was not a very good idea, to say the least.

I remember going in to Tate's office with Wheeler. Tate was not happy, for he had first read of the invitation to Gates, as we had, in the *Campus*. The consequences of allowing Gates to speak in the existing atmosphere were clear, and idealistic as I was about the freedom of speech which must be allowed, yea encouraged, I could see that Tate was already agonizing. Much time and energy would have to be put aside for this, and maybe crucial support lost. Tate did not leap up with joy, eyes ablaze at the challenge; but very soberly he decided to stand behind the students' invitation to Gates, because he believed that the students should have the right to invite the speakers they wished to hear on campus and that "the true is affirmed and the fallacious exposed in a free enterprise of ideas." So he stood with the students; and he persuaded Eugene McElvaney, his shield and buckler to the downtown community, to stand with him.

And we all stood there and took a bloody beating. The principle held, but those months until the event were terrible. Tate was ridiculed and vilified. He didn't seem to mind that, or he bore it well; what he minded through that time was all the other things we were not getting done because of it.

I remember no one, save myself, more shocked or numb at the time of the assassination of John F. Kennedy in Dallas than Willis Tate. He had gone down to the Trade Mart, waited, then come back to campus. I remember sitting in his office that afternoon. Never had I seen him so quiet. One vice-president kept wondering endlessly and absurdly whether we should cancel the football game Saturday. Someone else wondered if it was a larger plot, if we should restrict all students to their dorms. When Tate finally spoke, it was to tell us to be calm. I retreated to my office down the hall, writing draft after draft of a passionate speech— quoting Kennedy, quoting Frost—for him to deliver, to say to us, to give to the media.

Then at our Memorial Convocation I remember more disappointment than appreciation at the president's words to us, for he brought no more drama to the situation than was there. And in his way he outlined a plan for various commissions to investigate the quality of life on our campus and in our city: this was an absurd act, he seemed to say, the center must hold, we must come to know ourselves, our future is our true concern.

Tate the statesman again, conciliating his beliefs with a hoped-for better reality; and though it hardly suited my need or mood then, the positive seed he planted that grim day, as Mrs. Grimes suggests, continues to bear practical and positive fruit today.

In 1965 the SMU chapter of the American Association of University Professors nominated Willis Tate for the prestigious national AAUP Alexander Meiklejohn Award, "for significant action in the support of academic freedom." For years, from the first, he had defended academic freedom (by whatever name) in all its ramifications on and off the campus, to his trustees and to the public, often then turning around and challenging his faculty to understand that freedom and its terms and not to abuse it. When he was named recipient of the Meiklejohn Award, he characteristically arranged for me, who had fought some of these battles with him, to go to Washington to be on hand for the presentation. I have two impressions of that occasion that will never leave me.

Somehow Willis tore his trouser leg just before the ceremony. With great aplomb this distinguished figure walked upon the stage and gave his address to the AAUP with a great rent down the side of his britches, much massive All-Southwest Conference leg exposed to scholarly view. And the speech he gave was very much his own. The professors assembled were somewhat amazed, for they heard no ringing words from a fire-eater who had been down in Texas hitting his trustees and the honky public over the head with a stout academic-freedom shillelagh. They heard a gentle, reasonable message from a president who seemed almost to wonder how the award could have come his way. Tate dwelt on how supportive his trustees had always been. He had been able to do whatever he had done only because of the dedication, understanding, and support of his trustees and the generous attitude of the public in Dallas.

I chewed that over as I carried the Meiklejohn Award home for him on the seat beside me on the plane; this collection shows, in several places, that what he said to the AAUP was his true conviction.

Here he modulated a moment of personal triumph to reach out to those whom the judges making the award might mistake for the enemy. But there was no enemy; or, in the best Platonic Augustinian-Emersonian terms, ignorance, lack of understanding, was the only evil; an educator deals with that.

Then I remember, as a faculty member, opposing Tate in the 60s on an issue involving a speaker invited by students to the campus. I thought it was the same issue that we had stood together on in the Gates affair; I thought it was the lesson he had taught me. But this speaker was Timothy Leary, of drug fame, and I found that therefore the issue was different for Tate. It was a moral issue. Leary was morally dangerous, dangerous to students. My point here is not who was "right" on this issue. Certainly I took an absolute stand. (Leary never came, for whatever reason.) The argument aside, I was then impressed, and am now, at the care the president took to hear my views and the views of others— alumni, students, trustees, faculty. We were a concerned community; there would be no overtly arbitrary decision. After an all-night discussion, when I had led a faculty charge at the president which may well have been unfair to him at its sharpest points, I remember the president and the chairman of the board of governors, himself about as amenable to Leary's coming as to the abolition of the oil depletion allowance, coming over to thank us on the faculty for the expression of our views.

That caring about and at least in some way taking into account the ideas of others, that sharing of concerns and responsibility that led to SMU's "Shared Governance" system, was always a hallmark of the style of Willis Tate.

Finally I remember Tate's last great contribution to his university, in a time of shock and consternation and immense mistrust of the powers-that-be, when for reasons never formally given Paul Hardin was forced to resign as successor president to Tate. Tate had become chancellor, in cooperation with the fair young new president searched for so ardently. Now he was in the painful position of coming back as president, to hold things together while the search for a new president went on again. Which he did. Came back, the old tackle off the bench, like the legendary Blanda going to save the game with a field goal in the final minutes. And played it out. It was not a situation he created, or relished, certainly; but, given his record, what can only be called his *love* for SMU, there was no doubt that he would do so. And once more the center held. And we can hope and trust that we are together again, and back on the course whose aims and aspirations this university has so steadily held.

Much more can be said of Willis Tate, and will be said.

Much of value lies in these pages, which do more than I have been able to do so briefly to illuminate his priorities and concerns, to delineate his strengths, to suggest his frustrations and even failures. That he often seemed to the observing eye simpler, less complex than he really—humanly—was may be because of the singleness of purpose that always animated him.

If you read these speeches, you will find a mind dealing not only with specific problems and issues in one particular university but a mind open to and assessing the larger issues that marked his time. He never ceased trying to come to terms with the imperatives of higher education in its best tradition as he understood it, never gave up the effort to make SMU embody the timeless values that he held and that were as real to him as sunshine or rain, never stopped trying to assure that his university would be relevant to its time and place.

Emerson says, in that same essay quoted earlier, "A man is relieved and gay when he has put his heart into his work and done his best."

So must it be for this good man Willis Tate, of SMU.

MARSHALL TERRY

Dallas Hall, SMU
Dallas, Texas
January, 1978

PART ONE

Views

CHAPTER I

⊙╼╾⊙

Southern Methodist University
And the Space Age

INTRODUCTION

THE DEMANDS OF THE SPACE AGE made it clear that higher education
was living in a new day, one few presidents and fewer faculty committees were prepared to deal with. How to live through these years without losing opportunities to build a great faculty and yet maintain its
traditional role as an autonomous institution and an independent critic
of society was one of the great questions emerging for SMU during the
late fifties and early sixties.

The leadership of SMU and the industrial community of Dallas
clearly understood that any region in the United States which failed to
provide intellectual atmosphere, trained minds, and supporting institutions would become subservient to the intellectually advanced regions.
The time to build graduate and research capabilities at SMU had clearly
arrived.

The desire to have SMU become a university in the fullest sense,
however, predates the coming of the space age. The move to take SMU
into graduate education and research activities beyond the Masters level
began under the presidency of Umphrey Lee (1938-1954). President
Tate's planning took up where his revered predecessor had left off. Leaders of Dallas industry and SMU formed the Graduate Research Center,
Inc. on October 14, 1957. This center was designed to sponsor graduate
education and research at SMU. Between the founding of this center and
the incorporation of the Graduate Research Center of the Southwest in
April, 1961, a number of crucial questions surfaced for SMU. Could
SMU become a great scientific and technological research and graduate
study center and still not sacrifice its traditional liberal learning under-

3

graduate core? Was SMU to become a Cal Tech of the Southwest? Was SMU to benefit as a university in this pressure period for graduate programs and research, or was SMU to be used and its own leadership and resources drained by drift or design to serve other developing institutional concepts? None of these questions were in sharp focus early in President Tate's tenure at SMU. They were to come into focus later, however, with clarifying certainty. By 1962 it became apparent to President Tate that the conflicting ambitions of the Graduate Research Center, Inc. (to sponsor research at SMU) and the Graduate Research Center of the Southwest would not yield faculty development at SMU. President Tate knew that deficit budgeting, which had become a fact of SMU life during the late fifties to sustain a precarious momentum in faculty development, could not continue without a more precise understanding of SMU's particular purpose.

Strong forces have to coalesce and press before any deep institutional self-study, reevaluation, and planning can occur. Those forces included President Tate's own concern that SMU's future was being determined, not by SMU, but by outside forces. The joint study of SMU in 1961-62 by SMU and the Division of Higher Education of the Methodist Church added weight to the need for a major self-study. Transition is not a condition within which an educational institution easily understands its own purposes or finds the stability requisite to that achievement. Yet transition in the present and the foreseeable future was a major fact in the early sixties. President Tate was concerned about whether SMU had the capability of self-definition. Could SMU organize its leadership resources and channel the direction of rapid change to serve SMU's institutional purposes? Was SMU prepared intellectually for such leadership?

President Tate took the initiative in 1962 to lead SMU into a major self-study involving faculty, students, administrators, alumni, trustees, friends of the university, and educational statesmen outside SMU. The president assumed the responsibility of appointing the chairman of the Faculty Planning Committee, which he considered the most important committee in the entire planning process and from which he expected to receive his best intellectual and academic thinking. President Tate named as chairman the teacher-scholar whom he considered to be SMU's most broadly educated and most eminent scholar, Dr. Albert Cook Outler. This particular choice gave a clear indication of the president's concern that SMU's historical purpose not be scuttled but be placed in the context

of the late twentieth century and be given full and relevant new life.
Thus the Master Plan began. By May, 1963, it was completed and
adopted by the Board of Trustees. It defined SMU's clear intentions as a
private, liberal arts–oriented university, with selected professional schools
and graduate programs. The academic year 1963-64 was declared a
preparation year, with the new plan formally beginning in September,
1964.

The president's views during the period between his inauguration in
1955 and the drafting of the Master Plan in 1963 very often expressed
his concern that SMU was in a transition period. He spoke on the nature
of a university, the special dimensions of a church-related university, and
the urgency for Southern Methodist University to be clear about its
special purpose and mission.

The Fourth Dimension of Christian Education

*Speaking at the inauguration of Jack Stauffer Wilkes as the new presi-
dent of Oklahoma City University on March 6, 1958, President Tate
declared his understanding of the additional dimension a church-related
university must bring to higher education.*

IT IS NOT BY ACCIDENT that the Methodist church engages so actively
in higher education. In a very real sense, the Wesleyan movement began
on a university campus when John and Charles Wesley were at Oxford.
In our own developing history, the frontiersmen had hardly arrived before the Methodists were cutting logs so that they could house a school,
an institute, or a college. Our tradition has been simple: that the search
for truth, conducted with honesty and skill, will reveal God and illuminate the deepest meanings in the teachings of Jesus Christ. We do not
enter the educational field with a dogmatic bias, for we suppose that all
knowledge, when tested freely by men of integrity, helps us to understand our Creator and his creation. As the accumulation of knowledge
tends to cause thinking men to see that God is at work, the details of
that knowledge help us to understand how he works—and how we may
work together with him.

On the western frontier, the church assumed that it was obligated to make education available to the settlers. We have been brought by science to a new frontier, on which we have an obligation to extend in depth the fundamental dimensions of education, dimensions which are essential to both the survival and the growth of a free people.

The first dimension is *quality*. All educational institutions feel the obligation to keep their standards high. In the main, the task of teaching large numbers of students through a general and specialized curriculum will belong to public colleges and universities. They are even now preparing for this arduous assignment so that the highest possible standards may be maintained.

We in the church colleges are going to have a different and difficult task. We realize that we cannot teach everyone or everything. We must come to admitting a smaller number of students of more advanced preparation and concentrating on the educational exploitation of their ability. A large number of these students will become leaders of tomorrow. Many of our church institutions of higher education have found that they must begin this assignment by elevating entrance requirements to select the students who are able to begin at a more advanced level. This must not be mistaken for arrogance or an attempt to separate the quick from the dead-witted. If we seek to pick the better-prepared students to learn in our classrooms, it is so that they can get on with their work by the side of others who are ready to advance in an atmosphere of concern for the individual student. This must be done with a conviction that quality education is custom-made and not mass-produced.

It may be that we will presently be getting a large share of the exceptional minds to be trained as leaders at a time when intellectual leadership may even be a matter of life and death for our way of life. It is important to produce hundreds of thousands of trained scientists who will do the ordinary work of science. Someone, however, must find and nurture a few hundred exceptional minds to lead them. Multitudes will man the laboratories, but a few must take the places of Einstein, Millikan, Steinmetz, and Von Braun, to lead them into the new world.

By now, we have come to know that our salvation does not rest simply in the hands of the physical scientists, although their work is causing us to marvel. Part of the dimension of quality is the broadening of man's mind to comprehend the other wonders of life. We need to lead each student beyond the laboratory to see also the wonders of literature and music and the sciences of behavior and philosophy. This is our only guarantee of democracy. We want him to be a whole man, not a hollow man. I recently heard a fellow educator say: "We have been greatly concerned with outer space, but the most important space in the world is the space between the ears." We want to fill that space with understanding.

Increasing the dimension of quality in education will produce leaders who have breadth of understanding. They will have truly a liberal education. A product such as this is essential to the preservation of the human dignity which comes from recognition of every man's individual worth.

The second dimension is dependent on that breadth of understanding: it is the dimension of *substance*. This means that a student is provided an opportunity to know not only *how* to do things but what he is really doing and *why* it must be done. Many institutions will undertake to prepare a young person to get a good job and to be a worthy provider. Dorothy Thompson recently observed that many parents today have been lured into a cultural trap. They have become more interested in having their children learn how to type than in having them know the eternal values of living. No one denies that our young people must learn how to make a living, but we believe that it is *our* task also to provide the kind of learning that makes the living worthwhile.

For a long time we have been living in the crisis some call a cold war. Since the cold war is now being fought in the classrooms and laboratories of the world, this has produced a latent hysteria. It is possible to miss the whole point of learning. It is possible to divert our efforts principally to the materialistic emphasis of science. I recently heard Dr. Roswell Barnes express the belief that the nation need not and dare not subordinate its destiny to purely technological objectives. He reminds us that more than once history has witnessed the irony of a people unconsciously assuming the cultural characteristics of the nation it has defeated in a contest of power. As a nation we could establish technological superiority and become captive to the very materialistic dialectic we abhor.

The dimension of substance begins in the curriculum and is nurtured in the classroom, but it depends ultimately on the dynamic relationship between those who teach and those who learn. This is why we talk so much about the need for good teachers and the low salaries paid our teachers. A good teacher is a special person with a combination of at least three qualities: earnest scholarship, humility in the face of unfolding ideas, and a desire to communicate facts and ideas so that students may better understand man and his place in the universe.

We rightly hear much about classroom design and construction. Yet the finest classroom, with all of the latest gadgets, is a scene of destruction if it is presided over by a dull, cowed, unimaginative academic baby-sitter without insight into the divine potential of each life before him.

The third dimension of education is *freedom*. People in general have not begun to face up to the postatomic world. In this kind of world, for example, some form of collectivism could emerge, coming under the guise of efficiency, making full use of the technological advances which have shrunk the globe. In all of this, the more slowly and tediously turning wheels of democracy could grind to a stop and the excitement of being an *individual* could become just a memory. Some voices cry out to demand public control of what teachers say to students, so that education becomes indoctrination with the approved ideas of the majority, allowing no tolerance for deviation. What a tragic idea, for our whole democratic system is the product of people with active minds who revolted against exactly this same proposal.

In our economic system we are familiar with the term *free enterprise*. This term describes a belief that competition will test business practice and ingenuity and that the individual with the most effective understanding and the most energetic effort will produce the most successful result. In business there is the term *risk capital*. Not every investment pays off; not every oil well drilled is a gusher. In a free economy there is a constant period of disappointment and failure, but we know that success depends upon the calculated risk. Nowhere does this principle work with as much certainty as in the realm of thinking. The dimension which we can increase is that of faith in the "free enterprise of ideas." Ideas must have free expression so that they can be stated and given consideration to see if they can stand up under the pressure of the competition of other ideas. This is why free education encourages students to read and discuss differing points of view so that they may learn to evaluate them. This is how we educate for individuality and uniqueness so that all men may be free. No American scientist would change places with a scientist in Russia. We have had evidences, however, of science captured and "sworn in" to achieve an applied materialistic goal with no deviation, no reexamination of presuppositions, no stepping out of line, no unique or individualistic approach tolerated. This has led to an era of anti-intellectualism in our country with loss of reason and rational, creative liberty. What price do we pay for this subservience? Shall we rule the world and lose our own genius or our ultimate freedom?

The "free enterprise of ideas" always involves risk and produces some nuisances. In the free climate of a free university, strange voices will be heard, weird ideas will be stated, and intellectual arrogance will sometimes be found. But it is worth the risk, since significant ideas come in no other way than through free discussion. Worthy ideas are born in the climate of intellectual competition. Thus, the "free enterprise of ideas" occurs only in a community where there is a climate of mutual trust, where educators are free to trust the strength of truth to endure.

These three dimensions must be increased: the dimensions of quality, of substance, and of freedom. We who support and participate in Methodist church-related higher education have, however, another dimension. Our fourth dimension, on which we have no exclusive claim, thank God, but which we are obligated to trust, is the dimension of *spiritual orientation*. No one will suppose that this means simply encouraging students to go to church or to have strong religious activities or to have a good religious emphasis week. We do make these resources of organized faith available because we believe in spiritual orientation, but the orientation itself is something quite different.

Our faith in a spiritual orientation is based on a *master sentiment* which is fundamental to our tradition. We do not test learning by some static dogma; we never have to argue with the discovery in the laboratory for fear it may violate some ancient creed. Instead, our tradition is that the free search for truth, by skillful hands guided by discerning minds, will produce an increasing understanding of the Creator. We do our work not from an intellectual bias but from a spiritual bias. This bias is our faith that all knowledge affirms God by making his nature more understandable to us.

We believe in Jesus Christ as a revelation of God's nature among men. But we have also found that the insights of his teachings are illuminated by the discoveries of thinking men who search out the details of man's relation to other men and of man's connection with the infinite.

Dr. Eugene Blake once recalled from his early education at Princeton the belief that liberal education should enable a man or a woman to distinguish a stone, a statue, a dog, a man, and God and to know the proper response to each. A man who uses a fine bit of sculpture for a doorstop is not well educated. A woman who treats her dog better than her neighbor down the street is uneducated. But most important of all, an education which does not teach men how to know God and properly respond to him is no education.

Our tradition, therefore, frees us to seek to reveal God through the extension of knowledge and to illuminate the teachings of our Lord. We also receive our imperative to extend knowledge and to transmit it from the very conviction that knowledge shows us more of Him to whom we have directed our ultimate allegiance. We know that knowledge becomes wisdom only when it is related to the ultimate and the eternal.

Change and Imbalance

In the rapid explosion of science and technology, President Tate believed that there was a great need for commitment in higher education to the social sciences and the humanities as well as to the sciences. On March 27, 1959, he expressed his views to the Southwestern Social Science Association.

THE HISTORIC ROLE of the social sciences is to find a way for men to live in harmony in a shrinking world community and to determine a strategy for applying a common hierarchy of values. We live in a new world. Any one of the following innovations and conditions would be enough to disrupt a century, yet we have had them all since World War II: the birth of the Atomic Age, which offers us chaos or unlimited plenty; the breach of the frontier of outer space; the global struggle for human freedom; the awakening of the masses of depressed people of the world, which has made us live in an age of rising expectations; the strides in man's efforts to master his environment; the jet age; mass communication, with radio and television placing us at the ringside of every world event. A major world problem of the next fifty to one hundred years is that of human survival in the face of mounting population pressures. It is reliably estimated that by the year 2000 there will be four billion people living on this earth. We must not be like the man who said, "My God! Something walloped me ten years ago! What am I going to do about it?"

We live in a world little imagined by our forebears and with no assurance of what it will be tomorrow. The only certainty we have is the inevitability of change. Instead of perpetuating stability, our schools, colleges, and universities have turned into launching platforms where our students are pushed out into a new, baffling, and untried world. Many leaders feel that perhaps the most crucial issue of our mid-twentieth century is whether we are willing and able to adjust our politics to the imperative necessities of our technical knowledge and material power. Social scientists are familiar with the principle of social lag. When the different parts of our society are disparate, there will be no awareness of the varying rates of speed of the different parts. The strain that exists between two correlated parts of a culture which change at unequal rates of speed can, however, be disastrous. We are in a lag now. While we can truthfully say that the deep social implications of our swiftly changing scene have not been fully understood, we must recognize at the same time that there has been swift and immediate response by man to this change. We call it shock reaction. There are demands for quick solutions in matters that by their complex nature resist immediate and simple answers. This is well illustrated in the pressures which higher education faces today, pressures which have created an imbalance in education. The 1958 Carnegie Report, in a summary description of this pressure on education, makes it very clear that even in such areas as engineering education the pressure is on our leading institutions of education in those areas to provide more thorough and higher-level education in the fundamental sciences.

There is pressure from civic groups. The nationwide demand for an increase in scientific education in our high schools and colleges has brought about the appointment of special committees on scientific education stemming from a number of civic groups. These committees are charged with the responsibility of urging the public schools and colleges to place stronger emphasis on scientific education in their classrooms. There is pressure from the federal government, especially from the congressional bodies. This pressure has resulted in the appropriation by the federal government of large sums of money to be spent on scientific research.

Of special concern to all educators is the shock of change to the individual. Rapid change brings crises which breed fear and a sense of being lost. In this present climate of what is still shock reaction, we need to bring our new knowledge under a value system consistent with what we as a nation and as a civilization understand to be important in life. For my purposes here, the sources and the nature of these values are assumed. It is their application which concerns us today. Not all knowledge has been used for the good of mankind. Knowledge can serve a dictatorship as well as a free society. A look at the past and present dictatorships in the world will verify that truth. The power which knowledge bestows will inevitably become a political tool, to be used by someone.

The particular task of the social scientist is to find a way by which a common hierarchy of values may be applied to life. It is the job of the social sciences to be the meeting ground where ideals on the one hand and knowledge of man's world on the other can meet in a supporting relationship. The social sciences underscore the truth that we live both in a world of man and in a world of elements. Social scientists have long noted that it took man a long time to become scientific about the subject matter with which the social sciences deal. Human beings are the first things to which a person is exposed in the real world, but they seem to be the last to be scientifically studied. The rapid growth of the social sciences is an indication, however, of the value our society is beginning to place on the necessity for such study. Our democracy is dependent upon a better understanding of human beings, individually and in community. Only in a democracy can we find persons who are permitted to ask embarrassing questions. Only in a democracy may citizens realize that all forms of human institutions are but provisional solutions to problems, just as science itself accepts its conclusions as probabilities and not as certainties.

We must ask questions concerning areas of living which are most impervious to clear thinking. There are many areas of our life which we will not, as yet, allow the searching eye of the social scientist to examine. Against this background of a world in rapid change and the varied, irregular response of man to this change, the college and university stand, striving to fulfill their reason for being. A university must know why it exists. A university needs to reexamine its total life in the light of its purpose. But this purpose must not be just something on paper. It must be an expression of both faith and conviction. Woodrow Wilson said the purpose of higher education should be the training of the young in American life for the nation's service. To Wilson, the nation was a society of men, not a totalitarian state, a "social machine having life." Education, according to Wilson, must be appropriate to, and the most important function of, the community.

A statement of the purpose of a university which I learned many years ago was simply that it was for the education of the whole man to live in a free society. In a college or university, liberal learning, of which the social sciences are a part, is not placed at the heart of the educational experience to teach businessmen business or to teach grammarians grammar. Rather, liberal learning should help each person bring to his total life the greatest possible assets of intelligence, resourcefulness, judgment, and character. Liberal education must include an intellectual approach not only to what is fact, but to what is lasting, what is beautiful, what is true, and how this must relate to life as it is lived.

One of the most challenging expressions of the life of the university is found in its curriculum. No longer should there be war between the scientist and the religionist, the pragmatist and the idealist, between discursive truth and revealed truth, between pure and applied truth. Both are necessary. They complement and stimulate each other. Peace, of course, does not reign on the curriculum front. There has been an age-long battle for a share in the limited time allowed each academic discipline to influence the life of a student. Innovations in curriculum have never come easily. We now live in an age when the physical or natural sciences are in the forefront. This has not always been true. Curriculum change is, therefore, mandatory and has always been so by virtue of the purpose and function of education. As a prerequisite of understanding the place of the social sciences, we must also ask prior questions about the humanities. The intrinsic worth of the humanities is to be found in their foundational function. They provide the perspective in which we view what is important in life.

It is to the social sciences, however, that we turn for help in the business of living. They give us an understanding of the human person in his various communities. Not only must the social sciences provide a reconciliation or synthesis between the materialism of the physical sciences and the dynamic values in the humanities. The social sciences must also provide a strategy—a strategy outlining how the forces of men can be harnessed to bring the full life to all in our world. For example, full employment and inflation have to do with biology, chemistry, physics, and all physical sciences. They certainly are factors relating to peace, welfare, and the condition of man's soul. Who but the social scientist can give leadership and wisdom in showing how and when and why these forces can serve mankind?

What does history say about the great sweeping movements of mankind's highest achievement or his most pathetic folly? A study of man has revealed to the social scientist the complexity of man, but also his essential wholeness. This fact forces us to come to grips with all of the forces which influence modern man, within himself and in society. Within a university striving to fulfill its reason for being, there are many helpful forces at work of which our total society is in great need. The university must be the champion of the rational approach so needed in times of hysteria and emotionalism. Within the university there is freedom to examine all presuppositions. This opens many doors for the social scientist who takes his responsibility seriously. There is the opportunity for the great synthesis which some describe as integration of all of the academic disciplines in the life of the student. This is perhaps one of the really great frontiers in education today. It is especially needed when seen against the background of the student's feeling lost in a world of swift change. Our undergraduates are serious and for the most part dedicated. They are, however, bewildered. They cannot find their way in a world that changes so rapidly and in which it appears that an individual must be destined by forces over which he has no control or of which he has no understanding.

Some voices must call for liberation and balance. Some synthesis must come between the discoveries of the space age and the everlasting values of our heritage. Some counteraction must be made to the crash programs now emerging in education. Some strategy must be found to allow an individual, made in the image of God, to live in harmony and peace with his fellow men. With time and careful, energetic, creative attention to our business, and with full awareness of our purpose, perhaps we can let the light of rational behavior, peaceful interaction, and proven values light our world. Achieving this, we will also be able to bring into some degree of balance the way we educate our young.

Intellectuality, a Life Commitment

It was April 2, 1960, Honors Day at the University of Texas in Austin. In his address President Tate defined the lifetime challenges for the person of high intellect. He warned of the difficulties to be encountered in a society where the mass mind makes individual thinking difficult and conformity challenges the creative spirit.

THE MOST SIGNIFICANT DISTINCTIONS that a student can attain are those of academic eminence, for the highest service the student can contribute to his Alma Mater is to excel in the intellectual pursuit. In a way we honor today all who at any time in man's intellectual seekings have brought their superior gifts of mind under the discipline of learning. You, today, join this illustrious group. By giving recognition and honor to you, we do homage to the role of reason and to commitment to the rational search for truth.

You bring to this hour a number of things. You bring the discipline of study. For some, learning has been easy. For most of you the achievements of this day represent long hours of diligent work. Your accomplishment represents a deliberate choice on your part to exercise the freedom of study. You have exercised this freedom in spite of distractions and by resisting the many things student organizations can think up for students to do.

What you *are* today reflects what your university has given you the opportunity to become. Your university has enabled you to acquire and to polish skills of inquiry; it has helped you cultivate the capacity to retain, to remember. It has taught you to have faith in the truth and to be unafraid to search for it. It has reassured you that scrutiny can strengthen many beliefs you may cautiously or tentatively have held. Your university has provided experiences through which there has been born, slowly but surely, a full-grown self, with the capacity and the will to think, to feel, and to act upon discovered truth. In all of this you represent, in the finest sense, the fulfillment of the purposes of this university.

Those of you who have keen minds and sharpened intellects, with training in methods of rational inquiry, are greatly needed in this age. You are needed to man the laboratories, to devise and build the hardware, to perfect the cures, to solve the dilemmas, to ride to the moon, to negotiate, to preach, to teach, to perform, to compute, to legislate, to judge. Never has the world been more impatient for or dependent upon trained brains. This is true not only in science and technology; our world of complexity and change also requires the best brainpower in the professions, the humanities, and the social sciences.

While our world desperately needs and depends upon the trained mind, I cannot say our culture loves the intellectual. In fact, the opposite is true. The thinker is always a threat to the way things are or used to be. The thinker is castigated. He is distrusted and feared. There is no honors day down the road. Great pressure is built up to make the thinker conform. This pressure brings loss of creativity and expression. We see this compliance complex within democracy itself. One of the long-recognized risks of democracy is that we may have the *tyranny of the many*. A free society may reject critical intelligence as a weakness. Blind will can triumph through sheer weight of numbers. When this happens, we have created a paradise of the *mass-mind*. A great deal has been said about the word *conformity*: conformity in politics, in the kinds of ideas we have; social conformity; economic conformity; the belief that we must not "rock the boat"; we must adjust. This state of affairs is also evidenced in the reduction of taste, culture, and education down to the level of the largest number. "If everybody does it, it must be right" is a popular thought covering not only what we wear but also what we think. Mass communication has turned out to be a great leveler of society's tastes and values. The very image we have of what a successful man is, what he looks like, the clothes he wears, the split-level house he lives in, how he climbs the ladder of business success, helps to bolster conformity.

Not only is the intellectual world made difficult by the heavy, dead-ening weight of mass mediocrity, but in spite of our desire to see the intellect used responsibly in all areas of life and our concern for rational choices, we live in the kind of world where not all choices are clean, clear, rational ones. The man of intellect will face the reality that the demands of a complex and revolutionary world, at home and abroad, are so bewildering that *a perfectly rational judgment is not always one of the clean options of a dedicated, rational man*. Nothing is black and white. What about missiles and the atomic bomb? How do they serve the safety and health, physical and psychological, of mankind? Their very existence and potential use does not represent a perfectly rational choice. Yet at this time we feel we must make the choice we have made in regard to this phase of our national defense program.

Even the undergraduate is now aware of the vast amount of knowl-edge now available for us to learn. Responsible students today realize that most of today's graduates come out of our universities too narrowly specialized for this uneasy and changing world. In this day of everex-panding awe and wonder, with the facts of life running out beyond our reach, it is with a great deal of caution that I speak to a group of stu-dents about our society and the future. It is, nevertheless, your world and your future. It will demand not only growing knowledge and skills but an attitude, a point of view, a commitment with some degree of ration-ality about life. Let me warn you, however, that this dimension of life is rough to live with. Such a commitment is not going to be easy to keep. It invites disillusionment, particularly if you do not realize that facts and reason do not always have within themselves a magic solution.

One of the true marks of the rational man is what John Keats called "negative capability." Some of you will recall this reference. In a letter to George and Thomas Keats written in 1817, John Keats, describing what he called "negative capability," said that it exists "when a man is capable of being in uncertainties, mysteries, doubts, without any irritable (that is to say, impatient) reaching after facts and reason. . . ."[1] In other words, "negative capability" is the ability to live in the middle of doubts and incomplete analyses, inquiries to which there are no conclusive answers. It is to live with no disillusionment about the possibilities of reason, with no doubt about the value of reason. You, the intellectual, are a person who can still demand the utmost of a situation and bring to that situation the will and the capacity to pursue the methods, the canons, and the temper of rational inquiry. The limitations our world places upon you do not excuse you, for you, being who you are, must seek the full limits of reason in every area of life.

Let me warn you, however, against the dangers of partial commitment. One of these dangers is the temptation to intellectual arrogance. Your performance in this university during the past few years ought not to put you in any mood of contempt or condescension regarding others. Life is not lived on an intellectual plane alone. Life consists of many other things: love, compassion, sympathy, concern. These qualities also make their contribution in giving life its deepest meaning. These qualities add to our motivation to act. They give courage to our convictions and add zeal to living. The test for every man, therefore, regardless of the limitations or brilliance of his intellect, is how responsibly he makes his decisions. In the face of this test, a man of true intellect cannot be arrogant. He must be humble. The more he learns the more he knows how much there is to know, and how little he possesses. I believe it was Thomas Huxley who once wrote: "Sit down before fact as a little child; be prepared to give up every pre-conceived notion, follow humbly. . . ."[2] One of the really great intellects of this century is a man now retired from my own university. He is a great Bible scholar. However, he is much more than that. He is a great person, a loving family man, gentle, an eager listener. He is beloved by all who know him. He is a great discoverer of the truth, but as honor after honor has come to him through the years, he has never been arrogant about either his achievements or the honors he has received. This humility did not slow him up or cause him ever to hesitate to bring his fine mind and his depth of insight eagerly to every opportunity for advancing the cause of truth.

Another danger to the intellectual is isolation. No true intellectual can shut himself off from others or pursue truth by himself. He must have a sense of community and be a man of action. He turns synthetic when he says, "I am a thinker, not a doer." In spite of the difficulties ahead, in spite of the roadblocks placed in your path by unthinking people, the world is crying out for the man of intelligence to use his special gifts for the good of mankind and to save our civilization.

This action will take many forms. You will save our civilization in your laboratories. Who can tell how and when the research in seismology will influence disarmament? Who can doubt that Einstein provided a new basis for modern scientific thinking and yet he seldom left his blackboard. Action may take the form of political leadership or research in the humanities, seeking to understand the great heritage of mankind. Action for others may be in writing or in the teaching profession where, in spite of the many frustrations, a person may bring to the classroom the unusual ability to communicate, to inspire, and to contribute significantly to the processes of learning for the young. Action may mean giving sound and sane community leadership in face of the rabble-rousers and the hate-mongers who are abroad in our day. The whirlwinds of hysteria are all around us. In a world of mass communication where the person who talks the loudest may become the one who is believed, it is crucial that the man of intellect also be heard.

Whatever decision you make concerning how you will use your intellectual powers, each of you is responsible for bringing to society your particular contribution and the intellectual commitment you are capable of giving.

How can we appeal to you, then, to sustain and make lifelong a commitment to the life of reason? Can we appeal to your sense of duty as a motivation for you to continue to be a person guided by intellect and reason? I am afraid such an appeal will not be good enough. Duty is never strong enough to keep a bright mind from fudging and using his intellect on all kinds and sorts of rationalizations. If you would remain faithful to the high calling of scholarship, of excellence, and of intellectual achievement, your motivation must come from knowing more and more the deeper satisfactions of the life of learning and insight.

One of the deep satisfactions of a continued life of intellectual endeavor I will call simply delight. It is sheer joy, which lasts and lasts. Someone has described this feeling as "the genuine upsurge of the human spirit." Many of you have heard the story of Archimedes, the Greek mathematician of around 250 B.C. He was concerned with testing the purity of gold. One day while taking his bath, as he noticed how his body displaced water, a method of testing for the purity of gold by specific gravity occurred to him. He sprang out of the bath exclaiming "Heureka! Heureka!" (I've found it) and without pausing to put on his clothes, he ran to his laboratory to make the experiment.[3] I once heard a philosophy professor refer to delight as the "aha!" experience of a student to whom meaning for which he had been struggling suddenly came. Not every person who makes high grades has experienced this thrill of discovery. Some may be just "custodians" who through drudgery have attained high honors. Others may have started out on the scholarly road as a compensation for lack of other qualities. Yet as they have traveled this road they did, nevertheless, experience the real delight of discovery. From that moment on, such students will never again be merely compensating. Others have come this road, experiencing delight after delight because, being who they were, they could go no other way. If you have experienced delight in any of these ways, then you have known the wine, the true joy of the intellect, and you can never be satisfied with less.

Another deep satisfaction to be found in a continued life of intellectual vigor is that you will discover you have become a *lover of truth*. You will love not just for the thrill of discovery alone, not just truth for its own sake, but for a deeper reason. You will know now, and have this assurance increasingly validated in laboratory and classroom and in the marketplaces of the world, that truth gives meaning to the ongoing processes of life. A true lover of truth will be aware of its boundlessness. You will know the rich rapport that comes to the vast community of scholars. There is a spiritual kinship for all who love and trust truth. You will come to see that in the majesty of truth is the revelation of God himself. My message to you, therfore, is: don't let your intellectual locks be shorn! One of the truly tragic poems of all times is, I believe, John Milton's *Samson Agonistes*. Samson has been made captive; he is blind and in prison in Gaza, laboring in a common workhouse. It is his loss of *physical strength* he is bemoaning, but the same experience may come to one's intellectual strength:

Ask for the deliverer now, and find him

eyeless in Gaza at the mill with slaves,
himself in bonds . . .⁴

This was tragic for Samson. It is even more tragic when the man of
intellectual strength allows himself to become a man in bonds. You will
encounter many forces in life which will attempt to *shear your intellectual
locks*. These forces are in society, and they are also *in you*. The preservation of the intellectual life requires never-ending struggle. The words of
the New Testament come with particular appropriateness here: "Every
one to whom much is given, of him will much be required. . . ."⁵

Much is expected of you because of who you are and what your university has provided for you. The world desperately needs what you can
give. The greatest fulfillment in life comes when *what you have to give
so abundantly meets what the world needs so desperately*.

The Tide Is Coming In

*As the 1962-63 academic year began, everything was ready for an
intensive year of planning for SMU's future. Committees and task forces
of faculty, administrators, students, alumni were ready to begin their
work for the creation of the Master Plan. Outside consultants in the development and administration of a university were engaged for on-campus
visits during the year. President Tate wanted to involve the entire SMU
community in this exciting year. He invited that participation at the
opening Convocation.*

MOST YOUNG PEOPLE have experienced the surf—the inevitable buoyancy of being lifted by the incoming wave, the sureness of it, the rhythm
of it, the force of it that knocks out your underpinnings unless you face
it and use its might. Southern Methodist University, at this time in its
history, is being lifted by just such an incoming wave. Hard and sure
forces are rolling in. Some of these forces are from outside the university.
Rapid change must be seen as just such a force. Today's generation of
students faces more innovations than any other in history. There is the
force of the whirling printing presses and the doubling of knowledge in

a decade. There is the force of our country's determination to survive, calling for more brainpower. There are the developing needs of our region, dependent upon trained, highly skilled manpower.

Some of these forces come from within our own academic community. These forces stem from our transition from a primarily teaching institution into a university with graduate and research capability. There is an atmosphere of expectancy and urgency. We have come into the full realization that we are a university of promise, but a university whose promise has not yet been fulfilled. This is not a casual, offhand judgment. As many of you know, we have been engaged in a number of revealing preliminary studies: the retention study to see why promising students fail and why good students do not return; the Methodist study to determine the factors of relationship between church-related higher education and the educational experience; the cost study to find efficient methods and realistic data on expenditures; and the study by our Prudential Committee and research consultant on the feasibility of and strategy of graduate studies.

We have come to realize that we have a new measuring stick to judge our quality. We can no longer compare ourselves with what we used to be or even with contemporary neighboring institutions. We must be judged against an ideal that represents the very best in higher education. In this newer judgment our performance falls short of our pretensions.

We come face to face with our highest challenge: to be an arts and sciences oriented university where the college becomes the core and foundation for all our selected graduate work and superior professional schools; to be a university of balance—a balance between humanities, social sciences and sciences; a balance between undergraduate and graduate work; a balance between basic and applied knowledge. We desire to be a university that will motivate the highest intellectual rationality and social responsibility; to be a pacesetting university in our region in such important matters as quality of libraries, selective admission of students, and the attraction of a superior faculty.

We have now come to the year of the Master Plan. It is now that we must find our sense of direction and the role and image of this university. Given the world as we now know it, we have to plan. It is particularly appropriate that we are doing this reexamination at the end of fifty years of our university's history and the beginning of our second half-century.

This, then, will be the year of the open mind. This will be the year of soul-searching. This will be the year of decision and commitment for our future. Every person in this university is a part of this process. We have available outstanding educational statesmen as consultants, but the burden will fall on the faculty, the administration, the students, the alumni, our dependable friends, and the trustees. This will not be easy. This kind of evolution causes pain and strain. It makes some people apologetic and defensive, including your president. Reexamination of anything is no easy matter. Even academic people have vested interests and like all human beings find it hard to be critical of their own activities. It is easier for all of us to look for scapegoats and external determinisms. Our planning will be difficult, for there are no pat answers to be found in the back of the book. Like America, the university is a dynamic idea rather than a system or sovereign unit.

Even if we do not find all the answers, we can establish a sense of direction. We will resist the temptation to deal only in vague theory and high-sounding verbiage. We will cope with curriculum revisions and recognition of superior academic attainment by both students and faculty. We seek more self-initiative and responsibility in learning. We will come to see how learning and faith, education and religion can come to a valiant alliance to bring fulfillment of our social responsibility for freedom, equality, and brotherhood. We will find ways for humane treatment of each other in which our relationships are carefully individualistic and intimate and are not mass-produced.

Above all, our ultimate concern, our sense of mission, our vocational calling as educators must center irrevocably on the *teaching-learning* experience. The only true and valid justification for our existence here on this hill is to foster the life of learning. This is primarily realized in the teacher-student relationship, not only in the classroom and laboratory but also in the library, in chapel, and over coffee cups. In this relationship, an initiation takes place. The teacher initiates the students into the ferment of ideas. This can be no casual relationship. It demands that the teacher love learning and have idealistic regard for the learner.

There is no place in this process for the egghead who has contempt for the student, just as there is no place for the sticky fuddy-duddy who regards the student merely with sentimental affection.

There *is* a place, as there always has been, for those who would lead out in unenforced but incomparable discovery, the discovery of insight which enables us to reappraise the past and open the door to the future, whether that be in science or history or art or philosophy.

The relationship between teacher and learner is, however, a two-way relationship. Because of this, we ask of students: What ought you to expect of a professor? If you take the stand that it is up to the professor to interest you, you are then tempting him to gimmickry. This is *not* the life of learning. The professor is here to practice his craft of arts and learning. He is here to initiate you into the great ferment of ideas. If the professor has done his homework, you are privileged to be present when facts come alive, when data move toward meaning; and in the process you come to self-understanding. But for this to happen, the student must set his own disciplines. The way you order your time, what you think and talk about are matters of your own choice. Although we are deeply concerned about your fulfillment as students, we do *not* intend to stand *in loco parentis.*

While the faculty may be regarded as the primary teaching force on this campus, they are not the only teaching force. A major role is left to the students who will educate each other. The first measure of the depth of the life of learning on the campus of Southern Methodist University may be a professor who has spent years of preparation, but a more accurate measure will be what you read and the kind of student conversations that are held in the dining rooms, the lounges, the residence and fraternity houses of this university. We all educate each other: faculty-students; students-faculty; students-students; faculty-faculty; and all of you educate the administration.

Holding to this central commitment to the life of learning, we now look again to the period just ahead of us, the period of intense reexamination and planning. In so doing, we are now under the judgment we have invited. We have chosen to expose ourselves to measures of excellence. We have said we want to be a citadel of the humanities in a period of great scientific and technological discovery. We have said we want to serve our nation, our region, our community in the great drive for intellectual responsibility. We have said we value the individual student as a person of worth in his own right.

These are fine sentiments. They are worthy aims. But we have had enough of the golden glow. Now reexamination and hard work begin. We must look at ourselves through the eyes of our best and most loyal leadership; through the eyes of our visiting consultants who represent the best leadership higher education in general can offer. Out beyond this campus, there is a world starved for intellectual leadership. It is a world begging for the vigor and intelligence of youthful adults. This is our great "unfinished country," and it is the continuous miracle of America that this student generation represents the hope and promise of a country whose leadership in the world is only beginning. The tide *is* coming in!

CHAPTER II

The Years after the Master Plan

INTRODUCTION

THE MIDDLE SIXTIES saw a confluence of issues, each bringing its own pressures and demanding attention. Through research grants and facilities support, federal money continued to exert strong influence on the direction of educational goals. The civil rights movement, culminating in the Voting Rights Act of 1965, climaxed the drive for equality of opportunity for all Americans. The decade saw a decisive movement toward mass higher education, with an accompanying debate over egalitarianism versus meritocracy. From 1950 to 1970, the number of institutions of higher learning increased 41 percent. In the same period of time the number of students increased by over 170 percent, and the faculty by 95 percent. The future of the junior college movement finally became secure; the movement provided America with the most rapid and far-reaching expansion in education beyond the high school since the beginning of the land grant colleges following passage of the Morrill Act of 1862. The Vietnam War accelerated. Resistance to that war increased dramatically. Given the unprecedented growth and support of institutions of higher learning since the late fifties, the universities faced a major dilemma: should they assume responsibility as an agent for social change, or should they protect their status and financial interest in the governmental-industrial complex of America? This dilemma concerned the freedom of the university. How could a university, whose advances in learning create the producers of wealth and power, expect to remain free of that power? How could the university serve what the university conceived to be in the best interest of society?

In this pressure pot of growth, expansion, and special interests demanding to be served, a university survived and advanced by the maintenance of some degree of equilibrium within itself. It is not without reason, therefore, that one asks about the equilibrium of the university itself during the mid-sixties, an equilibrium soon to be sorely tested by the rise of student activism. Specialized schools in the university, with their able advocates and strong supporting communities, placed unusual stress on the university as *uni*-versity, its governance, its budget-making processes, and the accountability of its administration. Other schools with few or no advocates struggled for their share of support and influence in university decision-making.

An important additional factor in the equilibrium of the university during the mid and late sixties was that of faculty leadership. Those were the years of the "fast labor market." It was not always easy to find continuity and cohesion in faculty leadership. Loyalty to a discipline often superseded concern for the immediate institution and its traditional faculty-determined educational policies.

However strongly a university worked to maintain its interior cohesion, secure adequate support, and serve the larger society, in the decade of the sixties it found it extremely difficult to do these things alone. Costs increased dramatically. Whether seeking the tax or the philanthropic dollar or both, institutions of higher learning became increasingly nervous about continued support. In the late fifties the rallying call was for "brainpower." As the sixties moved forward the watchword became "resources dispersion." Thus, state planning for higher education was accelerated across America. State systems doubled in the sixties. Texas was among the states that established planning and coordinating mechanisms for public colleges and universities. The Texas Legislature included in its plans for higher education in Texas a mandate to recognize the importance of the private higher education sector. The *dual system* of higher education in Texas was formally acknowledged.[1]

Two simultaneous developments of great importance to private higher education and to Southern Methodist University occurred in the late sixties and early seventies. The Independent Colleges and Universities of Texas (ICUT) pushed for some form of "fiscal and educational meaning" to the call from the Texas legislature "to enlist the cooperation of private colleges and universities."[2] The end result was the historic passage in 1971 of the landmark Tuition Equalization Grant Bill (Senate Bill 56) by the 62nd Legislature. The enactment of this bill marked, for both public and private educators and educational statesmen in the Texas legislature, the climax of eight years of searching for ways to utilize to the fullest the resources of the state, public and private, in the interest of the higher education of the youth of Texas.

The sixties also saw the Independent Colleges and Universities become a national movement. It was now the clear intent of the private sector in higher education to *cooperate from strength* as all of higher education moved through the years ahead with a decline in enrollment, probable continuation of high costs, and a return to its natural state of austerity.

Southern Methodist University, engaged in implementing and financing its new Master Plan, felt, in varying degrees, the impact of all of these national and state issues. In addition, President Tate brought to SMU four new dynamic deans for the Schools of Law, the Arts, Business Administration, and Technology. The president saw this as essential to the building of a great faculty. There were times, however, when he wondered if the university could stand that much energy let loose on SMU's internal structures. He maintained, however, a sense of institutional integrity while all around him centrifugal forces were exerted continually by deans and their supporting trustees and publics.

The mid-sixties was also the era of the consortium. President Tate led SMU in participating in a variety of cooperative educational enterprises with neighboring colleges and universities. At the same time, he was working on the Governor's Committee on Education beyond the High School for the State of Texas. President Tate was committed to inter-university cooperation but he knew that SMU should cooperate from strength. The strong give, the weak take. He also believed that SMU, in selected fields, must have its own graduate programs to insure enrichment of SMU's undergraduate teaching.

The post-Master Plan years required President Tate to give special attention to interpreting SMU first as a university with a strong liberal learning core, and second as a private university in the *dual system* of higher education in Texas.

A Civilized Society

*President Tate spoke at the Commencement exercises for the gradu-
ating class of the Southwestern Medical School on June 3, 1963. He
expressed his views on the urgency of the need that professional education should be joined with the humanities for the good of society.*

ONE OF THE MOST URGENT QUESTIONS facing a civilized society is how
to remain civilized. With so much to learn, how can a person be competent in an expanding field of knowledge and at the same time be a
civilized person, aware of his inheritance as a human being, capable of
responsible citizenship? This issue is especially acute among those who
are involved in the sciences and those in the humanities. Anyone who
can read or write or pour elements into a test tube is aware of the intellectual civil war set off by C. P. Snow's lecture on "two cultures." I do
not propose to join the critics' debate over whether Snow is a good
novelist or not. He has, however, posed the question from which we
cannot escape. He has placed all of us into hostile camps: the humanists
who purportedly do not know what is happening in the world of science,
and the laboratory-bound scientists and technologists who are said to
dream of a scheme for the future but have little time for discovering the
roots of the past.

There is, by their very nature, a wide divergence between scientific
knowledge and humane learning. In the days of the ancient Greek civilization this gap could be bridged by a single person. In the intervening
years, knowledge has increased at such a rapid rate that it seems reasonably true that there cannot be a modern-day Aristotle. No one in today's
exploding scientific world can do what Aristotle did, or even what
Thomas Aquinas did with knowledge in the Middle Ages.

We *are* in Snow's two cultures, and we do not speak to each other.
But this is only part of the problem. Not only do science and the humanities not speak, but even within science the different specialties cannot
speak to each other. The fragmentation of knowledge is a fact that
scarcely needs illustration before an audience such as this. A crucial example, however, is to be found in our sophisticated weapons systems.
Here is a field which involves very specialized scientific knowledge. At
the same time, it is fraught with grave social implications. It is hard to
find a person who can comprehend all of the facets of modern weaponry.
To find such a person who is *also* humanely educated is almost impossi-

ble. Yet, so crucial is the issue of weaponry, no civilization today can afford anything less than a civilized person in this position of responsible leadership.

I recently came to know two persons, each living in a divided world and unable to see reality in its wholeness. One is a doctor-researcher-teacher, "hatched and developed" within the confines of the university without the maturing experience of private practice. In the judgment of a growing number of leaders in the medical profession, such a doctor treats not a person but "a medical entity," as though the doctor were an executive technician on a pinnacle, making decisions based on the summation of laboratory tests and charts. The other person, a minister who can read both Greek and Hebrew and who has spent the early years of his life becoming learned in the past history of the race, is one who cannot converse with the new scientific man in his congregation. Both of these persons are considered "educated," yet they cannot talk with each other. Our civilization cannot afford this kind of narrow education and the isolation it fosters, either for the doctor or for the minister. The truth has always been like a prism. It has to be seen from many viewpoints. As we take a close look at our exploding knowledge and at the growing demands for specialization, we can well ask ourselves: "Who has time or energy for many viewpoints?" Or we might ask as well, "Who has the time or the energy to be civilized?"

Our society must, therefore, face the question: With so much to learn, how can a person be competent in an expanding field of knowledge, and at the same time be a civilized person aware of his inheritance as a human being and capable of responsible citizenship?

There must be no oversimplified answers. A civilization with the intellectual ability to push back the frontiers of knowledge *must do so* or lose its intellectual vigor. We are in a period of unprecedented intellectual activity. It has been said that not since the invention of the wheel has society been so revolutionized as it has been during the intellectual creativity of the past twenty years. It is inevitable that out of our current emphasis on creative thinking and research there will come more and more highly specialized persons. While all of this must be encouraged, it must also be viewed with caution. Not every person is capable of making a valid contribution to the extension of knowledge. Yet today many are trying. Every person must be encouraged to make full use of his intellectual capacity. At the same time, institutions sponsoring research must carefully guard their standards. There is status in research today. There also are ready funds. This can lead to quantity without quality.

Perhaps no field of research is more in danger of a proliferation of research activity than is the field of medicine. Many of you may recall the recent widely circulated report in which it was stated that one out of every three full-time teachers in medical schools receives part of his income from research projects, most of them financed by the federal government. In 1940, this report continues, $45 million was spent for medical research, and it is projected that by 1970 $3 billion will be spent for this purpose. Twenty-nine percent of all new doctors now go into research and related work. At the same time, serious questions are being raised about the quality of that medical research. Quality thinking seems less available than adequate funding.

Educated people must talk to each other about this phase of our society's education. We must discipline our own fields, not to reduce research, but to insure its better quality.

The individual is not *just* a researcher or a scientist or a specialist. He is also a whole person, a member of a community, a citizen. His life should not be lived without regard to the social unit of which he is a part. The artist cannot divorce his activity from the general concerns of humanity. The businessman cannot say, "Business is business," and ignore the social implications of his decisions or leave the community problems to others while he tends his store. The doctor cannot be indifferent to the broader social pathology which breeds or aggravates the specific ills he treats. In dealing with this broader pathology, the doctor will find himself functioning primarily as a citizen and a member of a community. I know a young doctor who actively supports a nonpartisan forum group in his community because he feels the group's program lessens the neurotic fears many people have about the unknowns in today's public policy problems. He meets these masked fears in his examining room. To be a responsible person, he lives and works not in isolation but in full awareness of the conditions of the human family of which he is a part.

The researcher or specialist in any field, especially in the scientific fields, cannot be indifferent to the *use* his discovery is put to. Assigning responsibility is not easy, for in today's process of discovery many people contribute. The researcher who recognizes his human identity will, however, not be indifferent when his discoveries serve or injure mankind. The effective expression of this concern in our complex society is a great challenge to us as our research continues to move into the unknown.

The specialist who is also a citizen and a member of a community has regard for people. One of the greatest breakdowns in communication today has to do with our ability to see how things are with other people, to know what goes on inside another person. This requires that we be whole enough ourselves to be able to regard the other person as a whole human being. The attainment of this ability is the supreme challenge to us today, and I know of no other group of whom this is more urgently expected than the members of the medical profession.

We must so structure our institutions of learning, both lower and higher, that every person, regardless of his later specialization, will have ample opportunity to discover his social and human identity. Higher education must give to society worthy human beings and citizens *first*, and lawyers, doctors, engineers, ministers, teachers, second. Significant progress is being made in higher education in the direction of better and more humane learning for students who once thought only of acquiring skills or professional know-how. Over one-half of all American college students attend the large university complexes where the liberal arts college is at the center. We used to think of professional schools as separate institutions, with no organic or social or academic relationship to the larger educational institution, the university. In a comparatively recent development, however, professional education is seen more and more as an integral part of higher education. In many instances, this has meant no more than physical proximity. But in a growing number of universities moves are being made to increase the opportunity for dialogue between the professional and liberal arts faculties; to establish interdisciplinary and interprofessional seminars; to increase the liberal arts requirements for admission to professional schools.

We consider this problem to be so urgent at Southern Methodist University that we have restructured our university to make possible the latticing of liberal education and professional education throughout the baccalaureate years of our professional and preprofessional students. We have already achieved in our School of Law entrance requirements which insure that the law student will have taken the kinds of prelaw courses that will give him an opportunity to possess the liberated mind. Upon this foundation, then, the professional school works to turn out, in some degree, a civilized lawyer. Such a student then goes out into the world wholly educated to be a citizen and a member of the community first, and a lawyer second. Similar trends are being observed in engineering and in business administration. Two factors have profoundly affected engineering education in the last decade. One is the unusual complexity of engineering problems following hard on the heels of scientific advance. These advances demand new skills to acquire new knowledge and translate it into working systems quickly. A second factor of even more potentially profound effect requires that engineers no longer be considered as technicians for hire, but that they assume a more significant role in the affairs of mankind.

Such is the challenging climate of our civilization today.

We must become increasingly capable of orderly conversation about this, our world, in this, our day.

SMU's Fiftieth Anniversary

At Commencement in May, 1965, Southern Methodist University had completed fifty academic years. The university was founded in 1911 and was opened for students with the fall semester of 1915. Beginning with the Commencement of 1965, SMU opened a year-long celebration, marking the end of fifty years and the beginning of the second half-century. President Tate opened the celebration.

TODAY MARKS THE END of the first fifty years of the life of Southern Methodist University and begins a year of celebration. We have good reason to acknowledge with gratitude our particular heritage. The past fifty years have been significant years. That which is visible about this university has grown. We hope it will continue to grow. Our true strength, however, does not come from that which is visible. Our real strength comes from two sources: the basic presuppositions upon which this university was built, and the quality of leadership among the persons who first wrote down on paper and then lived out in teaching and administration what a first-class university must be. The tone and quality of this university was set at its inception. This university was committed, before its doors were ever opened, to a life of learning built upon high academic integrity, the unfettered pursuit of truth in a climate of freedom of inquiry, concern for every student and faculty member, and service to society as a source of intellectual, cultural, and spiritual energy.

President Hyer, SMU's founding president, never thought of this university as second-rate. When he chose our school colors, he selected the blue of Yale and the crimson of Harvard. He was dedicated to building out on a Texas prairie an institution of higher learning which would be first class. He chose the university's motto, *Veritas Liberabit Vos*, which has reminded many generations of faculty, students, trustees, and later presidents, the "the truth will make a free man of you." This dream of a fine private university attracted great men. President Hyer, in building the first faculty, showed uncanny ability to attract teachers who could teach and who had a concept of what a university should be. This dream of a university also attracted sacrificial support from many people.

We have drawn strength from these early leaders and supporters in good times and in bad times. They were always here when we faced crises, mistakes, depression, temporary discouragement, and loss of vision. The original concepts for this university and the men who made those concepts live have been the vital, unseen resources for the continuing, changing life of SMU. We owe them much. Today we acknowledge that debt.

The writer of the first Psalm was referring to man, but I believe that what he says also applies to institutions: "He is like a tree planted by streams of water, that yields its fruit in its season, and its leaf does not wither. In all that he does, he prospers."[3]

"*He is like a tree planted by streams of water . . .*" A tree is half visible. The unseen half of every tree is under the ground. But the continued growth of that tree, its leaves and its fruits, depends on the roots. Without roots a tree could look good for a while. If there is a decaying heart, however, the strong winds will soon destroy it. With healthy, well-fed, well-watered roots, many changes and storms can be weathered. In fact, the strong winds seem to give vitality to a healthy root structure.

So it has been with this university. Our heritage has never been to seek isolation and protection for survival. Rather, deliberate changes have been made by thoughtful pruning and grafting. Our roots are healthy after fifty years of life. They are resilient enough for us to face new interpretations of our basic presuppositions regarding a private, church-related university in our dynamic Southwest. It is always difficult to know to what extent a university accepts the substance of the past; it is difficult to know when to break with the interpretations of the past; when to let life continue; when to prune in the face of dying or unproductive members; when to graft new life upon the growing, thriving institution. In

all of these moments of decision involving change, we know that the
strength of the roots of this university will give nourishment to old and
new life alike.

In that faith, we move into our second half-century.

A Partnership:
Public and Private Higher Education

*SMU's leadership held the firm belief that society benefits when some
institutions of higher learning are state controlled and others are privately governed, and that competition is a waste of the tax and philanthropic dollar. On March 14, 1969, after the completion of the report
of the Governor's Committee on Education beyond the High School and
its acceptance by the Texas legislature, and six months after the final
report of the Liaison Committee on Private Colleges and Universities
was presented to the Coordinating Board, Texas College and University
System, as charged by the legislature, President Tate made a statement
on the question to the Lions Club of Dallas. During these six months of
1968-69, a public debate was taking place concerning the merits of
establishing a public university in Dallas to be attached to the University of Texas System. The establishment of the University of Texas at
Dallas was authorized by the Coordinating Board in December, 1968.
The new university was funded by the legislature in 1969 and opened for
students in September, 1970.*

*The first part of President Tate's public statement summarized the
formation of the Governor's Committee on Education beyond the High
School; the creation of the Coordinating Board; the formation and work
of the Liaison Committee on Private Colleges and Universities; and the
charge by the Texas legislature that both public and private higher education be used to help the state of Texas meet its full responsibilities for
the education of its youth. The remainder of the statement follows.*

NEVER BEFORE in the history of Texas has the state ever explicitly
charged the private colleges and universities with their share of responsibility for the education of the youth of the state.

Never before have the private colleges and universities been officially, publicly recognized as holding a portion of this responsibility. I doubt if I can adequately express to you what this has done to the private institutions of higher learning! We have made an exhaustive analysis of our resources and our potential. The entire private sector is now expected to deliver its share.

This expectation comes both from the Coordinating Board and from the Texas legislaure. They have clearly said that the dual system of higher education is an asset well worth preserving. The viable private colleges and universities in this state represent an investment in plant, equipment, land, and human potential which should be considered in any statewide educational planning. The Coordinating Board has acknowledged that this kind of cooperation is essential.

In this demand made upon us by the Coordinating Board and the people of Texas through the legislature, the private institutions of higher learning have had to say clearly *what their role could be* in this difficult, statewide shared responsibility. We have *both* looked at our state. What we have seen is a challenge to our *combined* efforts. It is a big job. The present enrollment in all colleges and universities in Texas, now at 373,700, will jump to 707,800 by 1980. The public sector will take the largest part of this increase. The private sector, while showing increased enrollment, will take a smaller percentage of the whole.

We who are citizens must bring our most careful thought and planning to this very necessary job. We who are educators have a special responsibility to help our state move in the wisest way to meet the costly educational needs of our youth, for it is an expensive job.

By 1975, Texas must provide $401 million in federal, state, and local funds for additional facilities for higher education. This is *new* money. In addition, there must be provided $404 million annually for instructional programs. This is double the present annual instructional costs. The members of the Coordinating Board, Texas College and University System, expressed for the state their great concern that ways be found to modify these costs. Included in their suggestions is the strong hope that the unit cost of education can be lowered through many forms of cooperation and the elimination of unnecessary duplication. We simply must find better utilization of the *educational dollar* which the people of Texas give, either through their taxes or through gifts to public and private institutions.

This is a challenge to both those who support the public sector and those who support the private sector. It should go without saying that there are some things only the state can do. No private university in its right mind would try to start a new medical school. There are also some things private schools, with their present extensive investments in educational resources, must continue to do under the freedom of their private governance. Public and private institutions of higher learning have always carefully avoided telling each other what to do. But they have been and will continue to be in constant conversation, *as they both stand under the judgment and support of the people of Texas.*

The private colleges and universities, in their report to the state, said that the revolution in higher education requires that we understand and respond to several important policy matters. Let me mention only one— that of the use of the college and university as an instrument of social change. Colleges and universities have been the birthplaces of major ideas for social and scientific development. In recent years, the nation's institutions of higher learning have been called upon more and more to assist in research concerning the problems of our society and to suggest solutions to them—in short, to become instruments of social and governmental policy and action. This is a staggering task. In light of these challenging responsibilities which face all colleges and universities in our state today, let me reiterate to you *the stance of Southern Methodist University in relation to cooperation.*

We, a privately governed university, will spend no time and no money on wasted competition.

We believe in cooperation.

We no longer approach TCU or Baylor or the University of Texas as if we were out on the football field. There *is* a place for gritting your teeth, bowing your neck, and saying under your breath, "It's them or us!" The place is on the football field or in some sports arena. It is *not* in the expensive, skilled business of higher education where top people are hard to find, laboratories cost a mint of money, and libraries take generations to build.

We believe in cooperation because we have engaged in it, and we know its worth. Beginning only as a tentative probing idea in 1963, the concept of interuniversity cooperation soon moved to formal organization in 1964. Even before the step toward formal organization, the various academic parts of five universities in the North Texas area were already experimenting in ways of cooperation. These five universities, later to be joined by five additional colleges and universities, public and private, eventually become what we now know as the Inter-University Council. Their ways of working together have grown. Their bold experiment in cooperation has encouraged other types of experimentation. Today there are dozens of such groups across the country moving into all kinds of cooperative programs, among public institutions of higher learning and also between public and private institutions.

Today, the University of Dallas, SMU, and TCU have a common core curriculum for the doctoral program leading to the Ph.D. in physics. This work is facilitated by the existence of TAGER, whose television studio is on the SMU campus. It is a unique privilege for SMU doctoral students in physics to be taught, by way of the TAGER network, by the president of the University of Dallas, a physics scholar. This kind of wise utilization of educational resources is essential if we are to avoid educational bankruptcy.

The entire SMU-TCU graduate engineering program and the SMU Honors COOP program in engineering and the Graduate School of Humanities and Sciences program in mathematics, statistics, and biology have almost 1,000 graduate students in remote locations, on other college campuses in North Texas and in industries. Of the courses, 84.6 percent come from SMU by way of the TAGER network. Of all the students enrolled in these courses, 86 percent are SMU students scattered across North Texas.

The question of how best to meet the growing demand for engineering students in our fast-changing technological society is a valid question. Some people think the answer is more engineering schools. Four new engineering schools have been organized in Texas since 1959. But there has been a *decrease* in B.S. degrees in engineering from 2,000 to 1,600 per year. Thus, *more schools do not mean more engineers.*

For the Dallas area, the answer to the problem of more engineers is to be found in quality engineering education. This has already been demonstrated by the sharp rise in enrollment at SMU's Institute of Technology this fall. Here, quality education plus innovative teaching is doing the job. In an area where science-based industries are growing, every engineer added to the work force in North Texas generates $200,000 a year in additional income to this region. "Metro-Tech," short for Metropolitan Institute of Technology, is an innovation in engineering education initiated by SMU's Institute of Technology this fall and carried out in cooperation with the TAGER network and other private and public colleges and universities. The Metro-Tech plan will provide leadership for the rest of the nation in solving metropolitan area problems through the effective marshaling of educational resources.

SMU and the Southwestern Medical School of the University of Texas offer an interinstitutional graduate program in bio-medical engineering, leading to both the Masters and the Ph.D. degrees. This graduate program has grown in number of students by approximately 140 percent in the last several years. The objective of the bio-medical engineering program is to provide competent graduate engineers with sufficient formal education in the life sciences to enable them to engage productively with colleagues from biology and from medicine in the solution of basic and applied life-science problems. Faculties of the two schools believe that students with strong engineering backgrounds can make worthwhile contributions in these areas, provided they are adequately prepared. SMU supervises each student's program, keeps all records, grants credit for all courses taken, and awards the degree.

One of the marginal cooperative ventures at SMU is the Gulf Universities Research Center, in which fourteen universities have an interaction in their geological and biological sciences program. SMU helped form this group and continues to participate.

One of the most productive and rewarding experiences of cooperation is taking place between SMU and the Southwest Center for Advanced Studies, known as SCAS. The program in the geophysical sciences is a long-standing cooperative program. SCAS scholars are adjunct professors in SMU's graduate Department of Geophysical Sciences. SMU, with its growing library resources, its campus, and its unique faculty has now become one of the top graduate programs in the country in the field of the geological sciences. It is with a great deal of pride that I report that I have been given on several occasions assurances from the University of Texas System in Austin that when SCAS becomes a part of their system this cooperation will continue.

The Space Sciences Research Center at SMU's Institute of Technology is a melding of the fine new faculty of the Institute and the faculty of the Atmospheric and Space Sciences Division of SCAS.

SMU has a cooperative program with the University of Texas at Arlington through which any faculty member from the latter university desiring to pursue work on a Ph.D. degree at SMU may do so without tuition cost to him. Through this plan a faculty member may, without uprooting his family, take time off from his teaching and continue his education, working toward the Ph.D. degree.

Much has already been said to the people of North Texas and particularly to the people of Dallas about the Inter-University Council's library network. All of the libraries of the colleges and universities belonging to the Inter-University Council are linked together in the teletype network. Through this network, we now have available for the educational institutions of the North Texas region a total of two million library resources. New material for all of SMU's libraries is being added at the rate of approximately 65,000 items a year. The Science Information Service, located in the new Science Information Library at SMU, continues to be a valuable resource for North Texas industries.

Southern Methodist University has clearly set its course. We not only believe in cooperation, we will continue to initiate it and give leadership to its accomplishment. But we believe we cooperate best from strength. We will serve this community and this state best by doing our job well and cooperating with others to enable them to do their jobs well.

Not the least of our responsibilities is our obligation to the city of Dallas, our oldest and most loyal supporting friend. The responsibility of SMU for this city was first stated in SMU's very first catalog when the first president of SMU, Robert S. Hyer, who served from 1913 to 1920, said: "A university situated in a large city is under an obligation to minister in every way practicable to the educational needs of the city. Southern Methodist University feels under special obligation to the people of Dallas." To this day, this commitment has not changed.

CHAPTER III

The Period of Student Unrest

INTRODUCTION

THE PHENOMENON of student unrest and activism was worldwide. It began in the United States in September, 1964, on the campus of the University of California at Berkeley. From that date until August 24, 1970, when a bomb explosion wrecked the Army Mathematics Research Center at the University of Wisconsin, Americans witnessed six years of student unrest, protest, and, on some campuses, violence. The years from 1966 through 1970 were the "hard" years. While there were many factors distinguishing the unrest in one place from that in another, a sense of a common history of the upsurge of student activism was to be found in the civil rights movement, the Vietnam War, and the draft with their concomitant pain and hostilities, plus the passionate conviction on the part of a significant number of students that their education was irrelevant.

President Tate's special concerns relating to student unrest during those years included his personal need to be sure he knew where *he* stood; the need for public understanding of what was happening; the urgency for faculty, as the group closest to students and the body most responsible for the university's primary function, to show alertness to the special responsibility the events of those years placed on the university; the need to be sure the SMU community knew who governed it and that the structure of that governance would stand under pressure. In addition, there was constant inner pressure on the president to be sure that his posture and bearing defused tense situations without denying the validity of student concerns.

Revolution on Campus

Student protests at Southern Methodist University remained non-violent. The distance between Dallas and the east and west coasts gave the university's leadership—trustees, administrators, faculty, and students —a chance to understand, deal with, and defuse the causes of violence. President Tate, however, was painfully aware of the anxieties in SMU's various publics over the meaning of the unrest among students. This anxiety was intensified following the week-long revolt on the campus of Columbia University (April, 1968), the closing of San Francisco State University (November, 1968), and the nonacceptance by the students of the newly elected president of Rice University and his subsequent resignation (February, 1969).

On March 13, 1969, President Tate made a major public statement on student unrest to the Dallas Pastors' Association.

TO BELIEVE there is no revolution on today's college campus is to be blind to reality. This condition makes some very clear demands upon educators and friends of education in our communities.

We must find ways of helping our youth to become healthily involved in the life of our country. These young people are going to be here in increasing numbers. By 1970, which is only nine months away, 47.4 percent of the entire population of this country will be twenty-four years of age and under! For some adults, this is fearful. For all adults, I trust it brings an enormous sense of responsibility. Every informed and thinking person in this country must know that these young people must be involved creatively and constructively in our country's life. We, as the adults in our society, have to be willing to see our world as having a shape that is not entirely right. We do not need to beat our breasts or clothe ourselves in sackcloth and ashes. We just need to be a little more honest. I know that in many ways many things are better. This, however, is not true around the world, nor in every part of our own country. Because our youth live in a day when all is known immediately through mass communication, we as adults cannot escape being asked, even pressed, for some explanation about the shape things are in. There *is* legitimate anguish among an alarming number of our students today.

To understand this anguish, we have to take an honest look at today's students. They represent the first generation of young people brought up in the time of immediacy. They are the first television generation. What happens in any part of the world is in their living rooms while it is happening, or at least immediately afterward. They do not have to wait a day or a week as we did in the parent and grandparent generations. They cannot understand why immediate problems cannot have immediate solutions. They are trained from babyhood to wait for nothing! They want action, now. They are conditioned to believe this is possible. Young people today are taught to ask *why*. Better educated than any group of young people in the history of the world, they are accustomed to questioning. From the time they are in their cribs, we help them develop their own imaginations. In a very real sense, we are coming to grips with what we have taught our youth to be. Their questions are painful. Someday, we hope, they will learn how difficult some answers are to find. In the meantime, we must face their questioning as honestly as we can.

Today's student has an obsession for "relevance." Many students feel and say that what they do during four to five years of college *must* have a bearing upon the issues of this day. They do want a more significant investment in their lives. Their studies and their out-of-class experiences must give them evidence to prove or disprove the matters at issue in their young lives *now*. They are quick to spot hypocrisy. They are idealistic with a passion which has not had an equal since the missionary days of the late nineteenth century. This means they are often openly critical of the education they have offered to them. As the problems of urban America spill over onto our campuses, as the disturbing issues of the war in Vietnam and the draft plague their young lives, the quiet progress of a conventional curriculum seems, in contrast, both unexciting and irrelevant. Rightly or wrongly, many students are complaining that they do not find in their studies material that provides them with significant answers and a meaningful education.

Mixed with this idealism is a demand for personal independence. Youth has always had an obsession for independence. Today is no exception. Now, however, it is a matter of degree. I think I can safely say that I have never known in my lifetime the intensity of today's students' desire for independence.

The obsession for relevance and independence on the part of many students today calls for delicate management. There must be some meeting ground between "riding with" the demands for individual freedom and meeting the basic requirements of a civilized society. There is a necessity for law and order, and there must be a willingness on the part of the individual to subordinate his desires to the value structure of his culture. We all must live within a system, and there is no reason why college students should be exempt from that requirement. Change must come through ordered processes. The recognition of authority in its rightful place is part of life. The highest freedom for the individual is dependent not on anarchy but on a society ordered and controlled by law.

All of this requires constant interpretation. The demand for dialogue with our students today is growing, not decreasing. In the process of dialogue, some students assume that what they have "said" is an "order" to the university. If you listen and hear them, some students assume you have agreed to do what they ask. We have to work harder to define how decisions are made, how students are to be involved as voting members of committees. We must also work harder to define areas over which students have *no* voting control, and areas where they *do* have such control. Through the Association of American Colleges, the administration has just completed a three-year study on the rights and freedoms of students. The American Association of University Professors has also joined in this "Joint Document." The document has been debated on campuses across the country, including our own campus at SMU. It was adopted by our faculty in April, 1968, as a basis for continuing SMU's efforts to develop principles and procedures specifically applicable to SMU. An editorial in our own free campus newspaper of January 25, 1968, stated: ". . . the 'Joint Document' includes many notions which have long been standing policy at SMU." We have a long history of significant student involvement in the affairs of this university. Students serve on university committees, run their own student government, maintain a free student press, and manage our student center through a student governing board, to mention only a few areas of involvement.

One of the most interesting meetings held by this university was the Curriculum Conference sponsored by the provost of the university last fall. The students came eagerly. They were in the large majority. A few carefully chosen faculty members also came. We discovered in this weekend conference that our top students and faculty agree on many issues. They discovered that the real meaning of "relevance in education" is that a student has a right to receive a college education which provides a rich background for his life; a college education which will feed experiences into his life at every point of future decision-making.

During the past two years, we have sharpened the discussion as to *who* the student is: son, ward, customer, second partner of a contract, junior scholar? We know, of course, that he is some of each. As our dialogue has continued with students, and as they have pressed for fuller participation in decision-making, the issue of authority has arisen continuously. Some of the things students want and demand seem to threaten what we think is sacred. Our authority is threatened. We as adults have to face the fact that whatever is comfortable and familiar tends to be wrapped in a cloak of sacredness. Change comes hard, particularly when it involves manners and morals. I think we feel threatened on occasion when our authority is not too well grounded and when the basis for our authority has not been well explained. As a result, our youth accuse us of being authoritarian. *Authority* is the power to expect and receive compliance. *Authoritarianism* is using power to require blind submission. It is easier to require blind submission if you are dealing with puppets. It is extremely difficult to get blind submission when you are dealing with bright young people who are learning fast about the world they live in. Of course, we do *not* want blind submission. Blind submission is contrary to the very purposes of education and destroys all we are trying to do in the whole complex of learning experiences. Authority, therefore, must be well grounded. We must be able to make our explanations understandable to youth. In some areas this is clearer than in others. The right, responsibility, and authority of the professor to grade the work of a student is, on the whole, unchallenged. Even so, in our growing, complex universities, the business of grading also needs interpreting. There is much criticism of grading being done, not by a professor, but by an assistant. "Testing" has to be useful, and its usefulness must be explainable. It is the university's unquestioned authority to set standards and in the final analysis to be responsible for saying who receives its degrees and who does not. We do this to our peril if we do not try constantly to improve our methods of judging and to interpret to youth the nature of the many ways they are tested and judged.

The question of parietal hours (visiting in the dorm rooms by the opposite sex) tests a university's authority at another level. How does a university handle this demand for freedom on the part of fellows to visit in girls' dorm rooms and vice versa? This university has said "no" to dorm room visiting while trying to provide more opportunities for privacy. Providing adequate space for privacy is expensive. Our income-producing buildings are almost all constructed with partial government financing. This financing carries with it certain restrictions on the use of the space in buildings. This takes away some of our freedom. I wish we could afford to provide for every student a place to live which would enable him to study undisturbed, with other areas where he could go for "breaks," play a stereo, raid the refrigerator. Our high school graduates get used to all of this in their homes. The university, however, does face certain limitations on what it can afford. Even so, we must learn better how to answer students more clearly. We must avoid clothing our regulations in vague words and moralistic tones. I know there are times, particularly when we cannot think of anything else to say, when it is good to be able to say, "It's a sin; don't do it." But for today's college youth who see our hypocrisies far better than we do, we should make a better case for our rules.

The university president cannot escape being the person responsible to the trustees for the total university. This carries commensurate authority. The president then becomes the primary authority figure on the campus. He is the "establishment" to rebel against. I have a sign standing outside my office door which was carried in a recent protest on our campus. The sign has Snoopy saying, "Curse you, Administration!" For some students and some faculty, "The Establishment" brings up visions of either a benevolent grandfather or an overstrict dictator. The role of the American college or university president is unique. He holds his office at the pleasure of the trustees who have the power to make his life easy or difficult, and who expect him to "run" the institution. He must not use his delegated power but must lead through persuasion a faculty whose cooperation is essential and whose members hold their appointments largely independent of the president. He must understand and be able to give a great deal of accommodation to the needs and desires of students. He is there to protect the freedom of students, not to permit license. He must interpret the purposes of the university to its many publics, all of whom provide support, financial and otherwise, to a university's growth and health. He must think about, write about, speak about, and work for *the whole*.

When a person is balancing a community of many divergent interests, he must study Ecclesiastes over and over again, especially that part which says ". . . there's a time for everything. . . ." In this particular time, I feel an unyielding pressure upon me to understand the nature of the student unrest across the country and on my own university campus, to deal with it from strength and in compassion, and to interpret this unrest to Southern Methodist University's various publics.

Who Governs?

President Tate had just seen the academic year 1968-69 come to a close. Student unrest continued. Demands were made upon the university by students, covering a wide range of issues. The president was convinced that all segments of the university—administration, faculty, students—must face together the question of who governs SMU.

He called two summer conferences on governance, with representatives from each of the segments of the university. His opening statement at the first governance conference on June 12, 1969, defines the issues as he saw them.

BECAUSE OF A LONG HISTORY of informal control and a wide-based, diversified decision-making structure, the modern university has found itself hard pressed to cope efficiently with the various pressures from within and without the academic community. While there will always be fundamental tensions between segments of the university, the strain of crisis on the American university today has exposed and deepened this power struggle, leaving campuses without resolute firmness and accountability to carry out its purposes and assumed responsibilities. *New* elements in the power game are now entering campus decision-making so that by now the trustees, faculty, students, alumni, parents, donors, government, foundations, and accrediting agencies are all clamoring for a unilateral decision-making authority.

Some of these power moves have been made over legitimate causes, and some have been merely game playing. Regardless of the reason, however, needless defensiveness and legalism have resulted in the watering down of the university's ability to act responsibly. This inability to respond has been interpreted by society as weakness and has generated a steady decline in respect for the institutions of higher learning.

While more fortunate than most (because, I believe, of the inclusion of faculty and students in the decision-making process), SMU has not escaped the power game. New and implied demands and requests have come from all sides. In each so-called "victory" (by students, by faculty, by trustees, by administration, by alumni groups) each of the other segments feels defeated or threatened. Let me give you a few examples of what I mean. There have been: (1) a recent revision of the bylaws of SMU to make explicit the authority of the president; (2) a recent request by the faculty to have representatives on the Board of Trustees;

(3) growing unilateral decision-making by the Faculty Senate and faculty committees; (4) a desire on the part of student groups to be the sole determiners in matters that affect their private lives, and to participate in decisions that go beyond their private lives; (5) for the first time, a resolution of judgment on the university received from the Alumni Association; (6) strong Greek alumni voices wanting decision-making power in fraternity and sorority affairs; (7) a new approach to funding individual schools via the special "foundation," which organizes donors and restricts and directs gifts; and (8) an expression of concern about all of this by members of the boards of governors and trustees.

While individually no one of these is bad or disloyal, collectively they leave the university and its policies confused and clouded. In the competition for power to decide, all segments become counterbalancing agents, and this reduces significantly the effectiveness of the institution.

It is my proposal that during this summer, in a series of meetings, we study the matter of *governance* in an open, honest, and unselfish manner. I believe we can quickly agree on common purposes and then come to some efficient procedures and adequate structures to make this university competent for the days ahead.

Before we list specific problems of accountability and the overlapping as well as the gaps in responsibility, let me remind you of another concern of mine as a background of our deliberations. One of the dangers in higher education today is the threat to *pluralism* in institutions of higher learning. Our democracy is enriched when we have colleges and universities of many different kinds. No university is equally competent in all fields. During the development of SMU's Master Plan, it was decided that SMU should *not* be patterned after another university but that it should have its own character and style. We have tried to define, to understand, and to establish ways of orderly self-renewal and change here at SMU. Our "image" becomes what our various publics see. While we are certainly concerned with what they see, as our very life depends upon our publics believing we are worthy, we are most concerned *to be* what we say we are. We must be flexible, progressive, and subject to improvement. Even so, no single segment of the university (president, faculty, students, alumni, or trustees) has the right to change unilaterally this university's purpose and goals. It is my hope that we can review what SMU *is* and find ways to protect it against erosion, from without and from within.

To accomplish this goal, decisions must be made this summer in the following areas: What kinds of students can best profit from the kind of education SMU offers, and how can such students be recruited? What kind of student body best enriches the educational experiences of all students? What kinds of residential requirements are desirable? How can we be diverse without polarization, excellent in peaks without undue imbalance, free with integrity yet understood and supported by our donor publics? Who makes and enforces rules and regulations, and will the system function in an emergency? Who approves student organizations? Who sets policies for publications? Who determines who is a guest on our campus and who is an uninvited outsider? Who determines if there are special needs of minority students, and who is responsible for meeting them? Who sets policies for fraternity life? Who handles demands, defiance, disruption—and how? Who invites guest speakers, and by what criteria are these decisions made? Should every segment of the university be aware of the university's undeniable need for private financial support? Who determines space and policies for the Student Center? What is the role and the future of the ROTC at SMU? Who disciplines the faculty?

As we move into our discussions on these many topics, I want to remind you that SMU is moving into one of the most important capital funds campaigns of this university's life. All of higher education faces the danger of a backlash among its alumni, interested persons, and the general public. SMU is no exception. For SMU, this backlash is due in part to the misunderstanding of situations that have recently received wide publicity. The real danger, in the long run, of adverse publicity or actual disruption is the potential lack of future support. Let us not be naïve about this. Such an outcome could cripple SMU. Therefore, it is imperative that we think through our actions prior to implementation. A destructive incident could come close to being fatal. Any time a group or individual undertakes an action that gets public notice, that person or group is being judged as a representative of the total university. This is unfair, but it is a reality.

I believe that our university community must be unified and not polarized. This unification must be based on the clear commitment of each segment of the university to help provide a superior education for our students. This may call for some measure of trust in each other, and faith that we can work out some unknown eventualities together.

The Ground on Which I Stand

It was during the years of 1968-69 and 1969-70 that educational institutions experienced the greatest degree of student unrest. College and university presidents, always the most visible representatives of their institutions, became the most conspicuous. Presidents were simultaneously the most troubled and the most important in managing the present and shaping the future of the institutions of higher learning.

It was not without cause, therefore, that President Tate sought for himself, as president of Southern Methodist University, a firm understanding of the ground on which he stood as he faced a confluence of decisions. On July 7, 1969, he expressed his thoughts about this at a symposium on "The American University: A Public Administration Perspective."

IT IS NO SECRET that a university president does a lot of thinking about his job these days. For about a year I have been trying to formulate in my own mind exactly where I stand on the nature of higher education and what this means in terms of the many new areas of decision-making which confront me as the president of a university. This is not to say that I have waited all these years to formulate such a statement. It does mean that the pressures on today's university make it imperative that we be able, perhaps more able than ever before, to articulate what we believe is imperative for higher education in general and our own institutions in particular. The following brief statements represent the ground on which I stand today.

1. *I believe an institution of higher learning is a voluntary association.* All colleges and universities, whether public or private, are voluntary associations with their own distinctive purposes and standards. Scholars are invited to teach; they agree to come or they decline and go elsewhere. Their right to membership in the new academic home carries with it a commitment to the character of the university as they find it, and a willingness to bring their academic leadership to the institution's self-renewal and change. Students, after examining a university's offerings in the life of inquiry, choose to apply and be judged by the university's admission standards. If accepted they voluntarily enter. I recognize the fact that in our highly advanced technological society today, education beyond the high school is indeed a necessity for an increasing number of our young people. I am also convinced, however, that some who are now in

our colleges and universities should not be there. With the rising costs of higher education, our society will soon be forced to deal with the problem of the kind of education beyond the high school our young people need. Our junior college systems will no doubt help us find a fair answer to the varied educational needs of our expanding mass of youth.

2. *I believe in "institutional uniqueness" in higher education.* Our democratic society is enriched by a variety of educational institutions. No college or university can be a fully adequate microcosm of society. Each university must decide upon its own unique purpose, setting the limits of its services to higher education. Each university should be expected by society to stand by its own chosen character and to be responsible for its own commitments. One of the more valuable unique types of institutions of higher learning is the private college and university, privately governed and privately supported. All of higher education benefits from the *dual* system of private and public institutions of higher learning. The two types keep each other serving society at ever higher levels of accountability.

3. *I believe that creative tension must exist between the various segments of a university.* Each university is a delicate equilibrium of nonparallel, divergent, and sometimes conflicting interests, influences, and forces. The fundamental tensions between students and faculty, between the different faculties of the various disciplines, and between all of these and the administration must be explicitly recognized and kept constructive. Because the different members of the academic body have genuinely distinctive roles and offices, the health of the body depends upon the cooperation of each segment with the whole.

4. *I believe discrimination is immoral.* Human society is diverse. Any arbitrary discrimination against one group, however identified, becomes an attack upon the integrity of the whole. Each person, therefore, must be accepted and judged solely on his qualities as a potential faculty member or student without regard to race or color. We must seek constantly to find better ways of judging the abilities of all potential students so that all who can benefit from higher education will have that opportunity.

5. *I believe people should be heard.* It is one kind of achievement for each of us to become the kind of *person* who hears others. It is quite another so to fashion an *institution* that people can be heard within its structures. In a university a person should not have to offend the sensitivity of others in order to be heard. Every person has worth. That person is helped to walk in dignity when his worth is acknowledged, per-

sonally *and* institutionally. A university by its policies, and a university's members by their deeds, must support everything which undergirds human dignity. We must refuse to support those things which offend human dignity. Deciding what offends and what supports human dignity, particularly in times of great social unrest, is not easy. Under the facade of propriety and decorum, it is possible to cover up injustice. Propriety, however, must never be used to cover up. The concept of that which is proper and fitting in a university community must undergird a broad humane concern, a concern which includes a person's right to be heard.

6. *I believe the college years are very special years.* A college education is not the only passport to a meaningful life. It is, however, by definition a process, traditionally compresssed into a few years, in which energies are organized, skills and insights are developed to enrich and fulfill a person's life. In this process, those who teach know more than others; but perhaps more importantly, those who teach are critical, evocative, exemplary. They maintain a climate and a style of life that attracts others to participate, seriously and joyously, in the learning-growing process. Conceived in this way, all college experiences, curricular and extracurricular, are potentially decisive for the growth of the person. The education years at the college level, however, during which being a student is a person's primary vocation, are not to be thought of as ordinary, everyday life. These years take place in a special atmosphere whose primary purpose is to warm the mind and make it receptive. Some of life's experiences which can be too demanding and thus rob the vocation of the student can be postponed until the college years are over. For years the university has judged carefully the course loads of students who also work. The increased amount of time and energy now demanded of student leaders is raising some questions as to what is to be considered an equitable curricular load for active student leaders.

7. *I believe we all stand under judgment.* "A deed is a deed is a deed." A university ought to be able to view each student as a responsible person and each student must accept the responsibility for his actions. This means quite simply that for every specific act there will be a response of some kind. This response must be expected. Final judgment comes on what a person does, not on what he meant to do or wishes he had done. Faculty, administrators, and students who participate in university governance are free to propose the course of action they think is best. But they are not free to decide if they are to be held responsible. Amnesty under certain circumstances is a form of dishonesty.

The university also stands under judgment. The success of educational institutions can be measured only in terms of the long pull. When a graduate is ten or fifteen years out of the university, the deep question too seldom asked and even less seldom answered with surety is: what difference did his college education make in his life? What influence made him socially sensitive or apathetic? What teacher made him come alive intellectually or killed his inquiring mind? The irrevocable right of the student is to believe his college education will matter in the long pull of his life. Under that right, a university is constantly being judged.

8. *I believe in freedom to learn.* One of the functions of a university is to assure freedom in a community of inquiry. This freedom, however, is a means serving a larger goal, the liberation of the human person. Freedom to teach and to learn is an indispensable means. Coercion, however subtle, however covert or hidden, must not be tolerated, for it denies the purpose of the university. Such freedom, however, has its price. The right of a university to be free is not a sacred right of immunity from criticism. All who are a part of a university have an obligation to the institution to protect, through responsible use, the freedom given to them. Only then can we sustain an open community where dissent is heard without censor and where disagreement and controversy are recognized as important ingredients in the life of learning. Reckless disruption diminishes freedom. It renders hypocritical the claim of the disrupters of their freedom and makes a mockery of freedom.

9. *I believe we must so govern ourselves that our best is made fruitful and our worst is promptly made better or discarded.* It is eminently desirable that each university devise a structure of governance that obliges and permits the community itself to be both the conservator of what the university authentically has been and must continue to be, and the architect of the change that is essential if the institution is to be relevant and effective at a time when rapid change is one of the few certainties.

To the General Faculty

Since President Tate's March 13, 1969, statement on "Revolution on Campus," the American public had, in April, witnessed violence on the campus of Harvard University. Now colleges and universities were mov-

ing into the school year of 1969-70, during which, it was later to be re-ported, demonstrations and protests of varying degrees of intensity oc-curred on 1,785 campuses, including that of SMU. The issue of whether SMU had an adequate governance structure was uppermost in the mind of President Tate as he opened the 1969-70 academic year. He had to be assured that this was also a concern of the general faculty, whom he addressed on September 2, 1969.

AS WE OPEN THE 1969-70 ACADEMIC YEAR, we face a very special mood of the times. This mood seems to be the result of a mixing of two fac-tors. During the summer months just past we were eyewitnesses to perhaps the world's most dramatic achievement in science and technology and in human courage. I refer to the "Moon Walk" proving that man, with a priority commitment, can do almost anything. In contrast, we have a deeply disturbed, impatient youth population, an unknown number of whom will be on our own campus this year. This past year the pressures have been constant upon all of us, designed to make us freshly aware of our country's domestic problems, our goals as a nation in relation to the world, and how these concerns should affect the education we offer.

Do we have an impossible dichotomy here between man's great step forward in science and technology and his dilemmas about life on this planet? Or do we have a mixture here of man's great skill and courage and his sensitivity to life, so supplementing each other that out of this tempering process there will come strength, resilience, and imagination from which all mankind will benefit? This is an appropriate question for a university to ponder. We of the older generation—that is, all of us over thirty—must accept a large measure of responsibility for the un-settled and at times chaotic world into which our young have been thrust. They are part of a society fearful of nuclear war, engaged in an unpopu-lar, unexplained war, and racked by domestic civil disorders. They are unwilling to accept poverty in the midst of plenty or the racial dis-crimination imbedded in our social fabric. They resent having no clear voice in shaping the educational and social institutions in which they must live and learn.

These are our youth whom we are expected to understand. Our stu-dents do come here to be taught by those who have earned the right to teach. In the context of a troubled society, this year, therefore, is a very special year for us.

We must continue to ask ourselves, as we prepare to teach and to serve on department, school, or university committees, or as deans and directors of special programs: "*What is the nature of the education which this university should provide for today's students?*" A university is above all a center of inquiry. Not just your inquiry, however. It is your responsibility to release the restless, probing, insatiably curious minds of those around you. It is your responsibility and opportunity to help students to order their spirit of inquiry. This releasing and ordering process is primarily and always the privilege of the teacher. This *is* great teaching.

Students can also help us to learn. Our ability to learn and learn fast is urgent at this particular time in the life of the American university. We must listen with sensitive ears to our students. We have many new technical aids to teaching today. Any teacher, however, who *can* be replaced by a machine, should be. The irreplaceable factor in teaching is individualization and personalization. Henry Adams was right when he said, "A teacher affects eternity; he can never tell where his influence stops."

Today I would like to make a modest proposal, which if taken seriously could be revolutionary in this university. I propose that you, with all deliberate speed, convert your committee meetings into sessions in which fundamental issues are proposed, discussed, and acted upon. The temptation to be engulfed in trivia is great for both faculty and administration. I urge that we convert all of our meetings into sessions in which the basic policy decisions are initiated, discussed, and acted upon.

Second only to our searching for the answer to the question of the kind of education we should be offering to today's youth is the urgent issue of "*How shall we govern ourselves?*" Today's universities are complex institutions requiring many specialized skills to keep them going. By tradition, universities are slow-moving. They are multi-based in decision-making, with little competency in meeting crises or time-pressured situations. Therefore, universities are also being identified as part of the crisis which faces our country. We in the universities are hearing sharp criticisms from students, from community leaders, from alumni, and from those scholars who study institutions of higher learning. In this crisis, the young, both white and black, are saying to us, sometimes timidly, hesitantly, politely, and sometimes rudely, obscenely, and violently: "We have been taken for granted. Nobody knows our names. This is our university. This is our world. Listen to us!"

While violence and duress are not acceptable from any source, neither is stubborn silence, or inflexible rigidity and inadequate response, on our part. This university has made significant progress in involving faculty, administration, students, and trustees in the governance of SMU. However, this wide involvement has been sporadic and without careful study as to where it is leading and whether it is adequate. We are now prepared to move into a major governance study this year. The purpose of this study is fourfold: (1) to enunciate a concept of university governance based upon shared responsibility among all segments of this university; (2) to identify those matters of governance that are primarily the responsibility of each segment of SMU; (3) to propose a means by which each segment of this university is given the authority, the accountability, and the mechanism with which to carry its primary responsibilities, and to provide means of appropriate review and checks by other segments of the university, for the good of the whole; and (4) to make a recommendation to the president for the implementation of proposed structures of governance.

We intend to take this study seriously. We expect everyone to be open to hearing others. We intend to see that this study is representative of all the major segments of this university. The study is not just an academic exercise with a report at the end of the year which will be placed in somebody's file drawer. This study will be made with the view of either reaffirming present governance or proposing to the Board of Trustees changes in our present structure—or both. While we study the way we should be governed, we intend to have a year in which our present governance structures, with some modifications, *stand* and *are made effective* by responsible faculty and student committees, and by the administration and the trustees.

We trust that everyone will work for that which is best for SMU and that none of us will be hung up on trivia or play power games. We cannot escape the fact that we *must* be governed in some form and under some structure. All of you are aware, I am sure, that there has been an alarming turnover in presidents of colleges and universities. I am perfectly aware that some turnover may very well be for the good of the institution involved. The rather large number of resignations, however, has raised in the minds of governing boards the issue of what kind of a person university trustees really want in the presidency. Some are looking for the "strong arm" person. Some are looking for men with "backbones." (All of this reminds me of some of the letters I received this past spring. My favorite letter ran like this: "Dear No-guts Tate: You ain't got the backbone of a worm." UNSIGNED.)

All of this reveals, of course, a fundamental misconception about the actual powers of the president. No president or administration will long exercise authority without the active support of the faculty. Faculty power is a fact, especially in those areas of most intense concern to students. Faculties must make the decisions about curricular matters; nobody but his colleagues can tell a professor that his courses are irrelevant to today's world. It is you, not the president, who dictates the extent to which "publish or perish" will determine faculty promotions and tenure. It is you, not the administration, who must determine the quality of admission and graduation standards. It is you who will decide whether new programs are to be offered, and whether contract research is consistent with the purposes of your scholar-teacher commitment. A president can have all the backbone in the world, but if his faculty fails to assume its rightful share of responsibility for the *real job* of a university, institutional spinelessness is inevitable.

The responsibility of the faculty is equally clear in judicial matters and in the handling of disruptions. We, as a university, must be able to put and keep our own house in order. We simply cannot afford to surrender this power and this responsibility to outside legislative or police authority. We must not surrender either the initiative or the ongoing leadership for any aspect of our complex list of programs to any outside authority, whether that outside force be from government or from the private sector. When trouble comes to this university *from the outside*, you as a faculty have a right to expect a strong, informed president to act. I hope you know that I am, first and foremost, your advocate. My strength, to whatever extent I possess it, is to fight your cause. This role is implicit in the bylaws of the university and is one which I take perhaps more seriously than any other as president of SMU.

At the same time, when there is a challenge to this university *from within*, I want a strong and wise faculty. I believe I know that you are, first and foremost, the loyal advocate of this university. If I did not believe this, I can assure you that my job would be quite impossible. This is going to be a difficult year. Your cooperation and your trust in the interest of our mutual responsibilities for this institution are both expected and appreciated.

To the Faculty Senate

On November 12, 1969, a detailed report was given by the president to the Faculty Senate on the circumstances under which a controversial speaker had been invited to speak on the SMU campus; the ambiguity of the process under which such speakers might be invited; the president's referral of the final decision back to the Faculty Committee on Organizations; and the charge to that committee by the president to clarify the university's ambiguous policy regarding speakers. The president then expressed, in the following statement, his concern that the faculty make clear the difference between the academic freedom of the faculty and the issue of free speech and an open campus.

I REASSERT THE RIGHT of students to hear all sides of any issue and acknowledge once again the historic responsibility of this university to provide a critical platform for the examination of all ideas. Freedom to teach and to learn are inseparable facets of academic freedom. The freedom to learn depends upon appropriate opportunities and conditions in the classroom, on the campus, and in the larger community.

There is much confusion, however, about the meaning of the sacred principles of free speech, an open campus, and academic freedom. There is no clear understanding of these terms, on this campus or in the larger community, even among educated people. These terms are used interchangeably. Free speech is protected by the First Amendment. However, every medium of communication which exists today makes its own modification as to what it will itself allow. Those who belong to the academic community of Southern Methodist University have a responsibility to see that the medium of this university is responsible; that what this university allows is educational in nature, done with a decorum befitting the kind of community we are, and appropriate to this university's purpose. This clearly means, to me, that this university places its own modifications on the meaning of free speech.

What is the meaning of an "open campus"? Does this mean the offer of a soapbox for any speaker? Or does it mean that *all issues* are open to be discussed by educationally competent people, selected by educationally competent people? I do not want a racist on this campus, offending our students, black or white. I know the faculty of this university does not want this either. I do not want obscene and perverted demonstrations which do a disservice to noble causes.

I know the members of the Faculty Senate have doubts as to who should judge the acceptability of speakers. Nevertheless, there is a line between license and freedom, and the procedures for determining this line must be responsibly established. This must be done by somebody. I hope it will be done by the faculty of this university.

Academic freedom is a professional freedom for the faculty to explore truth wherever the quest takes them. The student as a learner has great intellectual freedom and rights. But there *is* a difference between the faculty's freedom to teach and the freedom of anyone, no matter who, to speak to and for this university. A faculty member is screened and chosen for his discipline and his highly trained competence. He must constantly be exposed to challenge by his peers. He must be judged by his peers, not once, but constantly. By no stretch of the imagination can a faculty member say that the cherished academic freedom he has at this university can be given equally to anyone who comes to this campus for a day or a week without appropriate conditions carefully established and enforced with integrity by those responsible for the academic life of this community.

I challenge the faculty of SMU to know the *difference* between their hard-won academic freedom and the right and responsibility of any group or person to invite whomever they choose to hear on this campus. There is a need for clarification and discussion on these matters. Many members of our faculty are not in agreement with each other or with me. Maybe my ideas are faulty. Let *us*, here, as a faculty strive to come to a responsible and defensible consensus on these matters.

In fact, we are called to do this.

Most of our faculty members are familiar with the "Joint Statement on the Rights and Freedoms of Students" which is the official statement of three national bodies and, incidentally, a statement I helped to write. This statement, which was approved by the Faculty Senate and the Student Senate of SMU, clearly calls each institution to develop policies and procedures which provide and safeguard the "general conditions conducive to the freedom to learn."

This is the joint responsibility of the faculty, the students, and the president of Southern Methodist University. I will look forward to working with you on the development of the appropriate policies and procedures.

Kent State Memorial Service

Following the Cambodian invasion by United States troops on April 30, 1970, over four hundred colleges and universities closed for some period of time during the month of May following mass demonstrations against the invasion. On May 4, 1970, four students were killed at Kent State University during a confrontation between one thousand student demonstrators and National Guardsmen.

In the midst of tense feeling on the SMU campus, a memorial service for the four dead students was planned by SMU student leaders and held in Perkins Chapel on May 6. President Tate spoke:

MY FRIENDS AND COLLEAGUES:

This is a time of great remorse and sorrow. Every thinking person is pained and troubled. Those of us who treasure reason are heartbroken to see hate and violence rule the actions of men. We are appalled at the death of the four students at Kent State. We grieve not only for those who suffer under the tragedy of war, but also for those universities where anger and death have driven out trust and understanding.

Each of us is a child of God, made in his image.

Each of us must cope with shock, indignation, and sorrow.

Each of us must respond to our highest loyalties. For some it is a call to pray; for some a call to silence and meditation; for some it is a call for judgment and commitment. We hope for all of you it will be a call to think. To succumb to blind anger brings inhuman suffering and, as we have seen, even death. Some have suggested that an official day of mourning be declared, with a closing of all our programs and classes. Others wish to express themselves by renewed dedication to the academic preparation for a life of service to their fellow man. To many, such self-expression will depend on prayerful preparation for examinations.

We intend that each student shall decide for himself what his response shall be. For those who must express themselves with work, classes will be scheduled as usual. For those who feel compelled through personal commitment to forego class attendance on Thursday, there will be no penalty for such absence. For all of us, we trust, Thursday may become the symbol of our mutual concern. Let us pray:

Almighty God, father of mercies and giver of all comfort, deal graciously, we pray thee, with all those who mourn that they may know the consolation of thy love. Thou hast promised to hear thy children when they pray to thee. Help us now to pray; teach us what to ask for; help us to mean what we say, to love thee more, and to love the people for whom we pray. Through Jesus Christ our Lord. Amen.

Immediately following the memorial service, the students gathered around the flagpole which had become their meeting place in times of controversy. Anguish was so deeply felt and the passion to strike out so near the surface that even the wrong tone of voice might have turned disciplined anger into undisciplined violence. President Tate joined the group. Fielding angry, passionate questions, he said in a quiet voice:

I know you want to do something. I know you need to express how you feel. I am here to protect you against any intimidation in your right to express your deep feelings. I am sure you know that violence will damage the structure of this academic community. Each of you, however, will be protected from other students or outsiders as you express, in a nonviolent way, your hurt over this terrible tragedy.

On May 8, 1970, the following action was taken by SMU's Board of Trustees:

The Board of Trustees of Southern Methodist University wishes to express the sense of remorse and grief which it feels as a result of recent events throughout this nation. Both individually and collectively we share President Tate's concern both for those who suffer under the tragedy of war, and for those universities where anger and death have driven out trust and understanding. We all appreciate the manner in which the students and faculty of Southern Methodist University have chosen to express their deep distress over the crisis which faces mankind. The peaceful approach which they have taken in expressing their individual commitments reflects honor upon them and upon the University of which we are all a part. We, the Trustees of Southern Methodist University wish to reaffirm our dedication to a University where differing points of view can be defended without recourse to disruption, destruction, or violence.

> Board of Trustees
> Eugene McElvaney, Chairman
> May 8, 1970

Shared Decision-Making

Following the two summer conferences on "Who Governs?" called by President Tate in 1969, SMU took an academic year (1969-70) to study the possibility of developing a new shared governance plan. Faculty, students, and administration representatives developed such a plan, and it was accepted by the Board of Trustees in May, 1970, as a "contract between the Trustees and the various governing bodies" (without any bylaw changes). A Trustee-oversight Committee was appointed to work with the president and governance representatives as the new plan was implemented.

Educational leadership across the nation had just experienced a renewed outbreak of violence when in August, 1970, a bomb exploded in the Army Mathematics Research Center at the University of Wisconsin, killing a graduate student. In September, 1970, the Presidential Commission on Campus Unrest (the Scranton Commission) urged President Nixon to exert his moral leadership in healing and reconciling a divided nation. SMU was beginning a new academic year under a new shared governance plan which President Tate hoped would hold under stress.

The newly elected members of the various shared governance groups at SMU met at a retreat on October 9-10, 1970. The president opened the retreat.

THIS IS A NEW DAY in keeping a university alive and healthy. There has been an erosion of confidence. This erosion has occurred not because of anything you or I have or have not done. Issues bigger than our campus are causing anguish and unrest. The public in general is doing something it has not done before in my lifetime. The public is questioning higher education. Citizens are showing a loss of confidence in what we are doing. They are calling, not for a broader base in decision-making, but for tighter controls by a few. The publics we have to deal with are probably neither better educated nor less educated than those we have had in the past. Educators, also, are troubled and uncertain. The attitudes I hear expressed when I attend national educational meetings trouble me. These educators are wary of too wide a base for decision-making. They worry about whether students and faculty will give the time and energy required to make the decisions that must be made. Many presidents are saying, "The fight isn't worth what it takes out of me!"

I intend to lead this university in a real testing of whether governance can be shared. I am going to do this even though many think I am flying in the face of a terrible thing: distrust. I am beginning today under the assumption that I do not have any "Brownie points" left from the past. We begin a new day, here, this weekend.

We have a structure, a governance plan, which is worthy of being tried. There are some very vital parts of university life within the lists of functions of the governance bodies you represent today. If this governance structure is weak, it should be strengthened. If it is wrong, it should be changed. If it is reasonably effective, it can be considered for bylaw changes later. In any case, it is designed to be operative for three years, subject to constant evaluation and a major review at the end of the three years. I realize that some members of our university community are troubled over the fact that the president has a veto. I, too, am troubled, although I seldom use my veto powers. There are areas of university life, however, over which I have no veto. Curriculum, degree requirements, standards for admission are given by the bylaws to the faculties of the various schools of the university. There are other powers given to me by the Board of Trustees, and they expect me to use those powers when necessary.

It is much better that governance at SMU be handled by duly constituted groups. For this to happen, however, there are some very urgent needs each of us must face today. We must stand for a viewpoint without becoming the kind of advocate who beats down opposition. We need to restore some measure of faith in the other person's good intentions. If we enter every negotiation with loss of faith, it makes decision-making almost impossible. I do not mean that any of us should "give in" easily. I expect each of you to push hard for what you believe in. Building trust, developing the ability to negotiate, taking time to consult and inform, and, perhaps most important of all, learning to listen with sensitive ears: these are the supreme challenges before us as we open this new academic year under our new governance structure. There is one high principle I hope you will all join me in living by: loyalty to the university over the interests of special groups. This is essential. I am going to give that kind of loyalty, and I am going to expect that kind of loyalty from you.

The University and Politics

At the request of the Daily Campus, SMU's *free student newspaper, Chancellor Tate expressed in the September 14, 1972, issue of that paper his understanding of the role of a university and particularly Southern Methodist University in the field of politics.*

IN ITS BROADEST DEFINITION *politics* means the science or art of conducting political government. Because it is both a science and an art, and because it involves the broad spectrum of those being governed, *politics is the art of the possible.* This involves give and take, contention, debate, organization, and "campaigning." Those who would become "political" are engaged in taking sides in politics. They are working to achieve what they understand to be the possible.

Many institutions in our society influence the people who "take sides" in politics. Some institutions exert their influence directly; others indirectly. It is, therefore, very important for our society to have institutions which will affect the thinking, feeling, and acting of our citizens, either directly or indirectly.

The university is just such an *influencing* institution. It is *not* a political institution or force. It is, rather, an educational institution. Therefore, the university as an institution does not "take sides." The university does not use its power and influence and prestige in the interest of a particular political "side." It does, however, maintain an open climate for debate for all. Every shade of political thinking can be found in a university's marketplace of ideas.

It is the university's responsibility, in fulfilling its function as an *educational* institution, to train independent, creative, rational minds, minds that can be competent to deal with the demands of the "public good" and "political life": voting, working for particular parties, running, and holding public office.

Every person who belongs to a university community should feel free to be political up to the extent of his or her inclinations. This is done as individuals, however, not in the name of the university. Southern Methodist University does not disenfranchise any person who belongs to its community. Individuals join other individuals and become groups whose purpose is clearly "political," to "take sides." When this happens, it is hoped that the level of public debate on great issues before the people will reflect the genuine search for truth which is a university's goal.

While SMU grants to all individuals complete freedom in the political process, so long as they do not exploit their SMU affiliation or relationship, I as chancellor have found it expedient not to become political. Because the chancellor is authorized to speak for the university, it is hard for many to distinguish between his own position and that of the university. I am, therefore, careful that my utterances are non-partisan.

Every election year is important in the life of our Republic. I urge every member of the SMU community to exercise his or her freedom as a citizen in any and all ways open to us in this democracy.

CHAPTER IV

Academic Freedom

INTRODUCTION

THE FIRST ITEM on the agenda of the Board of Trustees of Southern Methodist University in May, 1954, was to receive the report of the presidential search committee and elect a new president. This having been accomplished with dispatch, the board moved to the second item on the agenda, the issue involving a senior member of the faculty and the meaning of academic freedom. With equal dispatch, the board referred this problem to the new president. From that moment until the end of his presidency, Willis McDonald Tate never sidestepped his responsibility regarding the defense of academic freedom against criticism from outside the university or its abuse within the university.

What Is a University?

On September 28, 1955, Willis Tate stood before the Kiwanis Club of Dallas to defend his university. He was big. He was trim. He was forty-four years old and had been president of Southern Methodist University for barely eighteen months. Those were the days just after the Senate's censure of McCarthy, and political opinions were running strong. President Tate was uncomfortably aware that his faculty was being attacked. His libraries were being criticized. His university's teaching-learning programs were under fire. It was time to remind this group of busi-

65

ness leaders of the true nature of a university in terms they could understand.

ONE OF THE MOST DIFFICULT TASKS I have had as president is to interpret the nature of a university. First, let me mention a few things a university is *not.* It is not a football schedule. We love athletics and take pride in our teams, but after a loss on Saturday afternoon we are able to open on Monday without a ripple. You can have a great university without a football team, but you cannot have intercollegiate athletics without universities.

A university is not a school for juveniles. A university is in the business of adult education. We cannot shield or protect our students from controversy or the facts of life, for when they are young adults they are living in a grown-up world. We must not be afraid of their being exposed to different ideas, hearing bad voices or picking up a peculiar book. All fallacy, all untruth, has within it the germs of its own destruction. Part of the young adult's process of maturing and learning to think for himself is this grappling with all ideas. This is not a dangerous conception of teaching. It has been used by the colleges and universities since the beginning of their existence, and it has produced the most stalwart leadership in our American life.

A university is not a college. A university is composed of several colleges and schools. The object of a college is to teach, but the object of a university is both to teach and to seek out the truth in every form. This is the process we call research. A university's stock in trade is not only students but also ideas, for new ideas are the most important things in the world. All progress has come from shocking ideas. Columbus believed that the world was round, and this shocked his generation. Lincoln, as a young man traveling down the Mississippi, was indelibly impressed in New Orleans with the shocking idea that slavery must be destroyed. The Wright brothers entertained the shocking idea that men might fly, even though many persons objected and said that if the Creator had meant for man to fly he would have given him wings. Three of our newest ideas have come from the setting of a university campus. Nylon had its origin in some basic research of a university professor whose principal interest was satisfying his curiosity about the makeup of the universe. Einstein's mathematical calculations were most often carried out on a university campus, and his highly theoretical formula of the relationship of mass and energy brought forth the atomic age. I was recently shown the laboratory where Dr. Jonas Salk discovered his antipolio serum on the campus of the University of Pittsburgh.

We have need for many more new ideas. Cancer is still to be conquered. We must discover how to solve international disputes and relieve tension among nations. There is a great frontier in the field of mental health. We have yet to defeat the evil of prejudice. The causes of divorce are challenging us. Alcoholism is a major social problem. We continue to seek increased competence and responsibility in government.

How does a university produce powerful new ideas? It engages great creative minds. Such great minds are rare. We provide their security and, if possible, pay them a living wage. We give them tools and time to think and study. A university then nurtures the spirit of examining each presupposition by holding it up to scrutiny, in the belief that whatever we can do now we can learn to do better. A university provides an atmosphere of freedom for its scholars, an atmosphere that is conducive to creativity. Here is the real power and strength of a university. Yet to provide an atmosphere of freedom is most difficult, since there are many people who cannot trust truth. They do *not* believe in the American tradition of open discussion. They would like to shut off investigation or discussion of the controversial and prevent all delving into fields of vested interest. They seek to shut off free inquiry by an appeal to fear and through name-calling. For example, Southern Methodist University has been attacked for having books on communism in our library. Of course we have books on communism! We cannot train international lawyers and foreign missionaries without them, any more than a doctor can study medicine without knowledge of scarlet fever. There is actually a great difference between teaching and teaching *about*. One is dogma. The other is free inquiry. A university is dedicated to free inquiry.

Let me illustrate how hard it is to keep an atmosphere of open discussion and freedom from intimidation. Occasionally a flurry of protests about a program on the hill develops into a storm of criticism. Our telephones ring and the mail pouch bulges. The word has been spread that the university has a dangerous radical on the campus. The feeling is that someone has pulled the wool over the eyes of absentminded professors and the university is being duped. Last May, SMU had on the campus a distinguished psychologist and his wife. He was invited by the university. He is the author of a classic called *The Mature Mind* which is an able presentation of the problem of human adjustment. He was invited to discuss the role of the minister in psychiatric care before an audience of graduate students in our theology school. Because of some positions that this couple held in 1932 about recognition of Russia, pressure was put on the university to cancel the engagement. He had been "cited," we were told, for his past interests by a California committee. Now, we had access to facts. I cannot mention them all, as many of these reports are made confidentially to reputable institutions, but I can give an example. We found that after reviewing all the charges that had been made against this couple, the House Un-American Activities Committee found nothing even to warrant a hearing; and this fact is stated in a letter from the chairman, Congressman Harold H. Velde. Other government agencies, in letters in the university's possession, further praise the work of this scholar and note the use of his book *The Mature Mind* by the government itself.

Another example is the recent Labor Seminar held on the SMU campus. Our Executive Committee feels that truth and education are good for everyone, including labor and management. Several years ago permission was granted to a labor organization to lease our facilities to hold a seminar on human relations, techniques of supervision and government. This is good. We do not want to be a party to political pressure, however, or to have a part in political blocs to support candidates for office. This would make the university have a vested interest and endanger the freedom we seek. Therefore, when the Labor Seminar this year announced that its purpose was to organize political pressure, we had to review and refine our policy. Their definition of education was not consistent with ours on this point, and we think it cannot happen again. I do not want to labor this point, but my telephone has been ringing again, and the mailbag is a little heavier right now.

Tonight, one of our twelve informal short courses begins. We are proud of these short courses for the service they render to busy people who want to improve their working knowledge of various fields without college credit. The one which begins tonight bears the name "Freedom Agenda." For the eight evenings in the course, we have gathered as speakers and panelists six of our best professors: three from law, one from theology, one from speech, and one from government. Two local attorneys, one prominent leader of women's groups, and four prominent newspaper and magazine men will take part. These people are going to discuss the fundamental principles of individual liberties and national security. From the list of names of people doing the leading I am sure it is going to be done well. This is the university's program, financed by a registration fee. It is not financed by a grant, as some of the letters I receive say it is. The Junior Bar Association has been pressured to abandon sponsorship. I have been told that this is because of an attack on the author of a Freedom Agenda pamphlet called *Freedom of Speech* and the fact that a radio commentator does not agree with the Fund for the Republic, which subsidized the pamphlet. Many who call me have not even read the pamphlet, but they want us to burn it. Our speakers in this course are not being asked to follow any pamphlet. We do have the pamphlet in question and the others in the series entitled Freedom Agenda available if any of our patrons want them. In America we think adults should be free to read and talk about anything they wish.

A great private university is the last bulwark of freedom in America. It is the only guarantee of freedom for our public institutions of higher learning. Some would have the university shun discussions that are not popular or hush up the minority voices. I cannot help but wonder: if we were to do this and if your position were someday to be a minority one, then where would that position be given a hearing and consideration?

Every university realizes that there are risks involved in this freedom. One is the crackpot who takes advantage of this freedom to voice views that are weird or extreme to the point of absurdity. Another is a person popping off outside his field of competence. Still another risk is the exploitation by some of this free discussion for their own benefit or protection. We think it is worth the risks involved. To be sure of our democracy we must create and maintain a great university here and keep it clothed in the atmosphere of freedom. This is our contribution to America and to mankind and in the service of a creative God. With His help, we are determined to do it well.

In response to President Tate's defense of academic freedom, the Faculty Senate of Southern Methodist University resolved "to express its appreciation to our president for the educational statesmanship manifested by this courageous stand on one of the most important issues of our time, and assure him of our continued support in his goal to make this institution one of the great universities of our land."[1] A resolution of the faculty of the College of Arts and Sciences stated that its members "most heartily commend the President of the university for the courageous stand he has taken in behalf of academic freedom."[2] The SMU Campus, student newspaper, editorialized: "In the life of every individual or institution there comes a time to stand up against criticism for what is right. Such a stand was taken this week by President Willis M. Tate when he declared the independence of our university from the influences of groups which would limit the freedom of the university to teach or act as it thinks best. A university should be a place of light, of liberty, and of learning."[3]

The Marketplace of Ideas

During the ten years following President Tate's initial defense of academic freedom, he interpreted many times the meaning of and necessity for freedom of inquiry and expression on the university campus. He coined the phrase "the free enterprise of ideas" as especially understandable and used it before a wide range of business and civic groups. On May 3, 1966, at one of a series of Industry-Faculty luncheons, President Tate expressed further views on the free enterprise of ideas.

A UNIVERSITY is a marketplace. It is a marketplace for the free enterprise of ideas. Every person in this room, I hope, believes in free enterprise. This concept of freedom in the market means that every product and service must stand in competition with every other. This freedom has made our country great and developed the highest standards of living the world has ever known. This has been done because through competition the shoddy, the inept, the outmoded is exposed and replaced. This is fundamentally the *same* freedom as academic freedom dealing in the realm of ideas. A university produces and tests new ideas. Controversy is merely the competition of ideas. Such competition is necessary. This process is the way truth is validated and fallacy exposed. Therefore, academic freedom is the right of the faculty and the student *to inquire* into all ideas; *to express* the results of this inquiry; to have such scholarly inquiry and expression *judged by their peers*. In a healthy academic community, this judgment goes on constantly. This freedom is not license to be dogmatic or to teach what a professor pleases.

In order that we may discuss fully the ramifications of *academic* freedom, I want to mention another freedom our faculty has, although I will not discuss it. This is the freedom which the citizen has because he is a

President Tate on his inauguration day, May 5, 1955. Courtesy of the *Dallas Morning News.*

President Tate at his first Commencement, held in Ownby Stadium on June 1, 1954.

On the occasion of the 1957 Jno. E. Owens Memorial Lecture, given by former President Harry S Truman. Left to right: Gerald C. Mann, President Truman, President Tate.

Two SMU football heroes and their coach, a quarter-century later. Left to right: President Tate, former coach Ray Morrison, Gerald C. Mann.

At the founding of the Graduate Research Center at Southern Methodist University, October 28, 1957. Left to right: President Tate; J. Erik Jonsson, chairman of the new Graduate Research Center's Board of Trustees; John G. Pew, board member. Courtesy of the *Dallas Morning News*.

President Tate with 1958 Homecoming Queen Norma James.

or R. L. Thornton pre-
President Tate with the
amation of SMU Week
allas, on November 15,
. S. J. Hay, general chair-
of the 1959 Sustentation
aign, looks on.

Students present
President Tate with
a copy of the 1960
"M" Book.

The 1962 United Capital Fund Kick-off, sponsored by the Texas Methodist College Association, Rice Hotel, Houston. Left to right: Campaign Chairman R. E. "Bob" Smith, C. E. Musgrove, Bishop Paul Martin, President Tate, Mrs. Paul Martin, Bishop Eugene Slater, Mrs. Law Sone.

President Tate in 1960 with retiring Chairman of the Board of Trustees Bishop A. Frank Smith (right) and incoming Chairman Eugene McElvaney.

Joel and Willis Tate at home, in the late 1960s.

SMU's Jerry Levias, Bob Hope, President Tate, and Tate's grandson John Withers, Jr., at the Cotton Bowl in 1968.

President Tate with members of the Board of Trustees, November 1, 196
Fondren, President Tate, Eugene McElvaney, Bishop W. Angie Smith, Bish
Vandergriff, Charles B. Paine, Eugene McDermott, Albert E. Fincham, Ja
Hubert Johnson, Earl Hoggard. Third row: Gerald C. Mann, Marvin Boy
Paul H. Pewitt, George F. Pierce, Charles Schneeberger, Harry A. Shuford,
J. S. Bridwell, Cleo C. Sessions, Nuell C. Crain, E. Clifton Rule, Albea G
Bryan, Joe B. Scrimshire, R. W. Fair, Everett E. Jackman, B. C. Taylor, G

to right: Bishop William C. Martin, Bishop Paul E. Martin, Mrs. W. W.
loway, Phoebe Davis (secretary of the university). Second row: Tom J.
, Joe Z Tower, Mrs. S. E. McCreless, Mrs. J. J. Perkins, Mrs. C. W. Hall,
ilton J. Daniel, Floyd B. James, Jim Willson, Bishop W. Kenneth Pope,
Fourth row: Layton W. Bailey, R. E. "Bob" Smith, Mrs. Fred F. Florence,
J. Borger, Ennis B. Hill, C. A. Tatum. Fifth row: Alfred P. Murrah, Monk
Sr., Perry A. Rowland, Ira A. Brumley.

President Tate helps Bob Hope to robe for the 1967 convocation at which SMU gave Hope an honorary degree.

sident Tate and Mrs.
. Perkins, as Mrs.
kins cuts the ribbon
he 1969 dedication
he enlarged Perkins
ninistration
ding.

President Tate with
representative of the
Pakistan Students'
Association, 1968.
Courtesy of the *Dallas
Times Herald.*

President Tate and Mrs
W. W. Fondren at the
formal opening of
Fondren East Library
in 1967.

Charles and Robert
Cullum, co-chairmen of
SMU's 1969 Sustenta-
tion campaign, with
President Tate at the
final report meeting of
the campaign.

President Tate in the midst of student unrest on the campus, in May, 1972.

President Tate finds this poster outside his office door during the period of student unrest.

President Lyndon B. Johnson, visiting SMU with Mrs. Johnson for a reception in her honor on April 14, 1971, walks down the steps of Owen Arts Center with President Tate.

On the occasion of the visit of the Prince and Princess of Monaco, in 1971. Left to right: Mrs. Algur Meadows, Prince Rainier, Princess Grace, Mr. Meadows, President Tate, Mrs. Tate. Courtesy of Gittings Studios.

President Tate, April 17, 1970.

citizen. A person does not cease to be a citizen or lose his political voice when he joins an academic community. It has always been the policy of this university that its faculty, students, and staff are citizens and are expected to act responsibly as such. The university does not approve or disapprove of what its faculty members do as citizens. The faculty members are expected, in return, not to involve the university in their personal decisions as citizens.

Risk-taking, especially in the marketplace of ideas, is as common as are the risks in the business world. Not every oil well is a gusher; not every investment is a bonanza. What are the calculated risks? Some people believe that *students might be duped*. If they are duped in the university, they certainly will be duped outside of the university. We cannot rear them in cellophane. We have to develop within them their own powers of criticism and evaluation. It can be done only by doing it. Sometimes I feel like a father whose daughter is on her first date alone. I have heard some friends of the university express concern over *the problem of an academic man speaking outside of his field of competence*. An enlightened community must learn to distinguish between a professor's speaking in his field of special competence and his speaking as an ordinary interested citizen. There are also those who express the fear that *academic freedom gives protection for the crackpot*. Let me remind you that academic freedom is a *professional* freedom, given only to those who have been carefully examined by the academic community for their training and disciplined commitment to high academic standards. We rarely see examples of those who take advantage of this freedom. Finally, we always face the fact that some fear that *donors might be offended*. A university loses some support if it maintains a free campus. But a university also gains in support from other sources when it is known that all society gains when the free enterprise of ideas pervades a university campus. Certainly, no one should be rich enough to buy off a university, and no self-respecting faculty would work in one that could be bought.

The Meiklejohn Award

On January 28, 1965, the president of the SMU Chapter of the American Association of University Professors sent to the national AAUP a letter, accompanied by a sixteen-page supporting document, nominating President Willis M. Tate for the Alexander Meiklejohn Award in defense of academic freedom. The letter said, in part: "I and my colleagues at SMU feel that Dr. Tate's wise recognition of the overriding importance of freedom of discussion for the academic community has been a great source of strength to this privately financed university in a city where business leaders have sometimes been provincial in thought and sometimes intolerant. We believe that President Tate's actions during the difficult past year and in earlier years are in finest keeping with the purposes for which the Alexander Meiklejohn Award was established."[4]

On April 9, 1965, at their national meeting in Washington, D.C., the American Association of University Professors presented to President Tate, "for significant action in support of academic freedom," the eighth annual Alexander Meiklejohn Award. In his response, President Tate was reluctant to accept full credit for his defense of freedom for his faculty. Some who participated in giving him the award may have thought they were rewarding a brave academic leader who stood alone in defense of academic freedom. When President Tate accepted the award, however, he praised his trustees.

I SHOULD LIKE TO SAY a special word about our Board of Trustees. I, and the faculty, have always had the backing of the trustees as a whole on these issues. Never have I had to face a situation in which my official board did not understand the nature of an issue involving academic freedom or were in disagreement as a body about the course to be taken. There has never been a minority position or action taken in these matters by the Board of Trustees, and this has meant much to me. I think that we often fail to realize that, while an administrator or professor can return to his academic community where his position is understood and supported, lay trustees often must remain exposed to pressures of the outside community that are greater and more constant than those that confront us. I am grateful for the heroism of many members of the SMU Board of Trustees and for the inspiration they have been to me as they have demonstrated faith in the freedom necessary to the educational process.[5]

CHAPTER V

SMU and the Methodist Church

INTRODUCTION

SOUTHERN METHODIST UNIVERSITY is owned by the South Central Jurisdiction of the United Methodist Church. The Jurisdictional Conference elects the board of trustees of SMU and delegates to the members of that board the responsibility, under SMU's charter, of directing and sustaining the university. The jurisdiction's direct and indirect influences on the university have been exercised through the trustees elected to the board.

President Tate believed in church-related higher education. He believed that SMU should be owned, not just legally but in spirit and in solid financial backing, by the United Methodist Church and its members. In that spirit and toward that end, he worked continuously during his eighteen years as president to interpret the church's role in higher education in general and in SMU in particular. He worked through the sixteen Annual Conferences of the South Central Jurisdiction, through the Texas Methodist College Association, and through the Jurisdictional Conference and its executive arm, the Council. President Tate wanted local Methodist churches, their pastors, and their lay men and women to understand SMU as a university and to see SMU's special role in the intellectual world as a place where, in both curricular and extracurricular interests, attention is given to the verities of the Judeo-Christian tradition. He wanted the church to take pride in SMU's growth and accomplishments, and to support it in times of stress and challenge.

Through the years, President Tate expressed his views to many church groups—local, conference, and jurisdiction—on the importance of the reciprocal relationship between SMU and the church. He was also con-

73

cerned to interpret and support the importance of the voice of the church
on the campus of Southern Methodist University.

The Future Is Now

*Methodist laymen from local churches in the Texas Conference of
the Methodist Church came to the Lakeview Assembly, Palestine, Texas,
on September 20, 1963, for a retreat. One of their major concerns was
the need for more information about Southern Methodist University. As
citizens, many of them were aware of the rapid growth in the number
of public colleges and universities in Texas. They were also aware of the
claims such expansion would make on both the tax and the philanthropic
dollar. Where did the church's institutions of higher learning fit into this
changing scene? In June, 1963, Governor Connally's Committee on Education beyond the High School for the State of Texas had been appointed
and had begun its work. President Tate was a member of this committee.
Church lay men and women needed help in understanding the role of a
church-related university in light of the growing number of state colleges
and universities. Should higher education be the exclusive responsibility
of the state? If not, why not?*

IN SOUTHERN METHODIST UNIVERSITY'S MASTER PLAN DOCUMENT,
adopted by the Board of Trustees in May, 1963, there appears this statement:

SMU shall reaffirm with pride its relationship to The Methodist Church which
in its own best tradition represents a commitment to non-sectarian education;
SMU shall reaffirm to its sponsoring body the University's intention of being
a true university with all this implies in terms of authentic academic freedom, responsibility and dedication. SMU, freed from enforced secularism,
recognizes its obligation to provide a context for the informed and responsible consideration of the moral and spiritual dimensions of great human issues,
and to do this in a forum in which the truth claims of the Judeo-Christian
tradition are given full hearing.[1]

This is no idle remark to please a board of trustees or to please the
ministers and laymen who know that SMU is owned by the Methodist

church. This statement is carefully and clearly constructed because the writers of SMU's Master Plan are convinced that the day of church-related higher education is *over* unless we can give just cause for its continuation. Ownership of the land, the buildings, the franchise to operate an institution of higher learning, be it university or college, will not in itself give meaning to church-related higher education. The church must examine *why* it is in higher education today, and know the requirements for staying in it.

The church and higher learning have a long and significant common history. The community of learning within the larger community of men was slowly and painstakingly worked out over a period of more than a thousand years. The effort began with the early church fathers; it was continued and strengthened by the learned monks, and later still by the teaching clergy who lived and worked and gave themselves to the new universities of medieval Europe. It is interesting to note that in the early beginnings of institutions of higher learning it was necessary to establish them *in independence of both the church and the state*, neither hostile to them nor beholden to them. From this independent position, the men of higher learning could work freely with both state and church to spread Christ's kingdom. The history of this relationship is filled with periods both of cogent reasoning and of massive persecution. In the seventeenth century, Harvard College in this country, like the University of Paris before it, was to be prized as "a learned encampment of the militia of Christ." It was to be seen as the latest link in a long history of association between learning and the church.

The church's early concern in this country was especially for a learned clergy. Most of the teaching faculty were clergymen. These early colleges were only secondarily concerned with an educated citizenry, and not at all concerned with the commercial and industrial life of their day.

The period of greatest development in higher education in this country came in the four decades following the War between the States. It was during this period that the university as we know it began to come into full bloom in this country. While there were a few universities prior to the 1860s, most of the institutions of higher learning were essentially colleges. In the four decades following the 1860s, a variety of social changes set the pattern and pace of American life, extending into the twentieth century. A great complex of universities was a part of and helped to create this change. After the Morrill Act of 1862, better known as the Land Grant Act, state universities began to flower. Since the latter part of the last century, the justification of higher learning has been increasingly judged not by a teacher's evangelical calling as a member of the "militia of Christ" but rather by his contribution, in teaching-learning-research, to the great industrial and commercial sources of power for our individual and national life. That higher education, state, private, and church-related, is deeply involved with social and economic concerns of our society, we tend now to take for granted.

While some may say with satisfaction that higher learning has now been freed for broader inquiry and service, there is a haunting feeling today that the early concern of the institution of higher learning for moral and spiritual values is in need of revival. Part of the rationale for this feeling is to be found in the world in which we live. The enormous explosion of knowledge almost stifles the imagination. The cold war has given an impetus to scientific and technological learning never before experienced in the history of learning. All institutions of higher learning, particularly universities, public, private and church-related, are being pushed to develop the sciences and technology to the neglect of the humanities and the social sciences. This is being done through training grants, foundation gifts, industrial support, and community pressures. I do not mean to imply that the sciences and technology should *not* be developed. We must see, however, what is being left out and undeveloped. Last year, with the help of our senior consultants, SMU was developing a chart of costs for graduate education. This involved especially the number of faculty needed, the number of students to serve, fellowships required. Then we looked at the possible sources of support. There were many sources of support for engineering, physics, mathematics, but nowhere in sight was there any support for philosophy, religion, history, sociology. This kind of neglect is frightening.

It has always been easy for a college student to lose his moorings when pitched into the world of ideas. In the past, there was perhaps less danger that a college student's concept of God was *too little* for his new knowledge. In today's intellectual ferment, on today's college or university campus, the chances of a student's concept of God being too small has greatly increased. This loss of the source of values for life is tragic, both for the student and for the society which needs his leadership.

Learning is not safe without wisdom. Traditionally, the institutions of higher learning stood for *wisdom*, the church for *faith*, and the state for *power*. This division is of course too arbitrary for the thinking person today, but as I look at the broad spectrum of American life, I am con-

vinced that we would do well to review this division. If there is one thing
we want students to get from a college or university education, in addition to knowledge, *it is the wisdom to use it.* Most people will agree that
you cannot *teach* wisdom. Acquiring wisdom is a lifetime undertaking.
We do, however, want the search for wisdom to become a part of the
learning life of our youth. There are two ways in which we must help
students begin to search for wisdom. When we have fully understood
these ways, we will have come to know *the case for a church-related
college or university.*

First, we must see to it that students have knowledge of the wisdom
of the past. This means certain definite, specific things to me. I face this
issue every time I sit in a budget review committee. Providing knowledge of the wisdom of the past means that a college or university will see
to it that in a liberal education its humanities and social sciences are
developed at least equally with the physical and natural sciences. A student must be introduced to the questionings about life from the viewpoint of the poet as well as the biologist. Southern Methodist University,
in facing its responsibility as a church-related university, has described
its concept of the educated person in these words:

The aim of this university is to educate its students as worthy human beings
and citizens first, and as ministers, lawyers, teachers, engineers, buinessmen,
research chemists, etc. second. These double aims, basic and professional education, general and special, cultural and vocational, cannot be separated nor
should they be. The well-educated person is a whole human being. His intelligence and his practical interests interact in all of his major activities. The
rationalization of the scientist who shrugs off all responsibility for the use
to which his discoveries are turned, the rationalization of the artist who
divorces his activity from the general concerns of humanity, the rationalization of the business person that "business is business," are so many symptoms
of faulty education. The curricula of the university and its teaching processes must be so designed that its general and its special aims are carried
out concurrently and in relation to each other.[2]

Providing knowledge of the wisdom of the past means that specific
course offerings in religion and philosophy are as much required for a
liberal education as mathematics and English. All higher education, and
especially church-related higher education, must concern itself with the
ultimate aims of man; it must concern itself with the meaning of life.
Providing knowledge of the wisdom of the past means that any development of a doctoral program in a church-related university must include

a Ph.D. in religion and/or philosophy concurrent with doctoral degrees in economics or geophysics or engineering. Unless *we* provide competent scholars in religion to the broader field of higher education, there will be a void in this important area. Colleges that wish to offer undergraduate programs in religion need competent Ph.D. graduates to staff those programs.

The second way in which we help students begin their search for wisdom is more intangible. We must provide the kind of spiritual and moral ferment on our college and university campuses that will stimulate *creativity in wisdom.* There must be a breakthrough from what Galbraith and Tracey Jones have called "conventional wisdom." "Conventional wisdom" is found in the *known,* the *familiar,* the *acceptable.* Emerson in his now famous address to the Phi Beta Kappa chapter at Harvard gives great tribute to the wisdom to be found in books. But he urges students to realize that the writers of the wisdom found in books *were once students themselves,* living in another age. Today's students must find wisdom for today's living through more than books *out of the past.* They must find wisdom out of the ferment of life today. This means something quite specific to me as a university president. Finding wisdom in the ferment of college life means that a university or college must have a free, open climate of inquiry. We believe in the truth. The Methodist church has no dogma that need fear any inquiry in the laboratory or classroom of a good school. Truth is expanding, but as it is God's truth, we must seek it without fear.

Finding wisdom in the ferment of college life also means that the voice of the church must be heard without apology, with clarity and strength. A church-related university has no leader more important than its chaplain. No activity offered to students and faculty is more necessary than the office of public worship, freely offered and freely accepted.

Finding wisdom in the ferment of college life today means that in all areas of human thought and conflict a church-related university will bring to the campus strong personalities with insight, with reasonableness, with commitment to the verities of the Judeo-Christian tradition. There is nothing to which we give greater care than the voices our students are asked to listen to.

All of us like to play close to the liferaft, even university presidents. We are reluctant to swim too far away from what has become our source of security. In times of great change, however, what is safe, wise, secure is always in danger of obsolescence. We must educate our youth to be at home in the uncertainty of a turbulent sea and the unknowns of space. Youth must be helped to understand and reaffirm the great timeless truths of life within the context of the changing and the unknown. The church cannot afford to surrender this responsibility to the state alone.

I call you, urgently, to assume your share of this responsibility for our youth. I want you *to know* about your university, SMU. I want you to *take pride in it*. I want you *to own it in spirit* as well as legally.

The church is here to stay. Its higher education arm must be a strong, well-used, well-cared-for arm of the Body of Christ, the church.

The Plastic Character of the College Years

President Tate was not passive about the place of the church on the campus at Southern Methodist University. His views regarding the church on campus were: (1) the Methodist church expects SMU to be a good university; (2) such a university would include in its curricula offerings the scholarly study of religion; (3) the voice of the church would be heard on campus, not across the street. Provision for the office of the chaplain and of Religious Activities was and is a part of the university's budget. Other religious bodies, when accepted by the Committee on Student Organizations, have been welcomed on campus along with a wide range of other student groups. An ecumenical approach to religious activities among students is encouraged, paralleling their own denominational fellowships.

Regular University Chapel worship services, under the direction of the chaplain and the Faculty-Student Chapel Board, offer public worship during the university's long term. President Tate did not always understand the university's chaplain, nor did he always agree with him. One thing was clear, however. The president respected and protected the freedom of the pulpit. The president gave this freedom equal weight with the professor's freedom to teach. The chaplain, at times, might have preferred some desk-pounding over issues; but it took quiet, probing conversations for him to discover what the president thought as a Methodist layman and a university president. Such was the president's basic respect for the freedom of the pulpit. President Tate believed the church had an unusual opportunity on the college campus. He expressed this view many times, but especially on January 5, 1966, upon his election to the presidency of the Council of Protestant Colleges and Universities (later to be known as the Association of American Colleges). The statement was also used later to open National Christian College Day.

ALL TRUTH BELONGS within the purpose and power of the Creator, whether acknowledged or not. Perhaps one of the greatest needs students have is help in seeing the unity of truth, in understanding the relationship between a partial though none the less valid truth and another partial truth. This requires innovations in curriculum-building, such as interdisciplinary approaches to learning. This is the kind of responsibility a church-related college must recognize and pioneer in. It is also an opportunity in which the church-related college has *unique* freedom. Studying the interrelatedness of truth is not only educationally sound but spiritually maturing. We have a student generation looking for commitment, and seeking through commitment to find meaning for life. One of the major concerns *we* have, as church-related colleges and universities, is that students *do* find some meaning to life. There are many competing philosophies which seek to meet this basic need of students. Colleges and universities have within their halls thousands of students for whose ultimate loyalties these many philosophies are competing. Students are in crucial stages of maturation and development. It is this *plastic* character of life and experience which creates a unique opportunity for the church to communicate the Gospel.

How this is done is crucial. Such communication must take place in full understanding of what is influencing the life of the students. There must be understanding of the sociological, psychological, and personal forces at work in the life of the student during the concentrated period of time when the past is handed over to the present generation to be examined, changed, appropriated. Such forces are set in motion by the character of the world we live in and by both curricular and extracurricular experiences as the business of inquiry goes on. It is not the purpose of this brief statement to spell out how the Gospel is communicated, but to define the unique opportunities which the church faces in these crucial years of the life of a student. These opportunities for the church are partially open but decidedly limited in the public college. They are *uniquely open* in the church-related college.

The Published Word and the Methodist Church

Southern Methodist University's library holdings were approaching the one million mark. Yet, for SMU's special needs, there were serious gaps. President Tate believed that the Board of Publications of the Methodist Church should assume a greater responsibility for the publishing of scholarly works by the great minds of the church. On October 25, 1966, he spoke to the Board of Publications on this subject.

SLIGHTLY OVER FOUR CENTURIES AGO John Foxe said:

We find this aforesaid year of our Lord 1450 to be famous and memorable for the divine and miraculous invention of printing. . . . Notwithstanding that man was the instrument, without all doubt God himself was the ordainer and disposer thereof. . . . By printing tongues are known, knowledge grows, judgment increases, books are dispersed, the Scripture is seen, the doctors read, stories opened, times compared, truth discerned, falsehood detected. . . . Wherefore Almighty God of His merciful providence, seeing both what lacked in the Church, and how also to remedy the same, for the advancement of His glory, gave the understanding of this excellent art of printing.[3]

As far as I know, no one has improved on this summary of the benefits of the published word. "*Tongues are known.*" There is nothing quite so provincial in today's close-knit world as the person who knows no language but his own. Most of us fall into this class. But this will not be true of our grandchildren, for we are spending thousands of dollars for books and magazines printed in foreign languages and for expensive language laboratories to accompany the published word in many languages. All of this began centuries ago when it first became possible to study another man's tongue through a printed book. The phrase "another man's tongue" has taken on a new dimension today. Words, even of one's own language, are often unknown. With the explosion of knowledge and the multiplicity of specializations, the meanings of words have many variations.

"*Knowledge grows.*" We cannot imagine a person acquiring knowledge today without the aid of published material, especially books. One of the indispensable parts of any advance in knowledge and new discovery of truth is that it must be published in some form and made available to others. The publishing of all research is a matter of great concern to universities today because of its increased volume and also because of the activity of the federal government in research with attendant security issues.

"Judgment increases." All human judgment is based upon that person's own knowledge acquired through personal experience and through reading. Most of us would have difficulty making any sound judgment on the role of government, foreign policy, taxes, the problems of aging, biblical criticism, to name only a few, if we did not have the published word to help guide us.

"Books are dispersed." I understand that the Methodist church's Dallas Cokesbury Book Store ships into this city over half a million books every year. This bookstore is only one of about a dozen major book distribution points in this city alone.

"Scripture is seen." This was quite a statement four centuries ago. Many people had heard about the Bible and had heard it read, but few had touched or seen the Scriptures. Before it was possible to publish the Bible in any quantity, a single copy was chained to a reading stand for the few who could come by, stand, and read. Yet today the Bible, thanks to the advances in the publishing field, is the world's best seller, with the whole or parts being translated into over twelve hundred languages and dialects.

"The doctors are read." The bright intellectual leaders of every age are the companions of every person who wants to know. When I occasionally look out of my office windows and see the students at the change of classes walking across the campus, I think to myself, "How could a student miss getting a good education at SMU when there are hundreds of thousands of mankind's best minds in the books of our libraries, just waiting to be read!"

"Stories are opened." The humor, the pathos, the philosophies of mankind, caught up in the most teachable language in the world, the story, has become every man's heritage.

"Times compared." Engraved over the exit archway at Pan America's International Airport in New York are these words from Santayana: "He who refuses to learn the lessons of history is forced to relive them." Without the published word, we would have a difficult time learning the lessons of history.

"Truth discerned, falsehood detected." This is done through a free flow of ideas and *not* through censorship. It has always been my firm conviction that truth will be discovered if there is an open library with books of all kinds, representing many viewpoints. Truth has an even

better chance of being discovered and falsehood of being detected if people can read and then discuss what they read in a free climate of inquiry.

The published word and the church have a long history of close relationship. We of the Methodist tradition share richly in that history.

Southern Methodist University is fast approaching the one million mark in its library holdings. We spend approximately three-quarters of a million dollars in budgeted money every year for our libraries, and much more through unbudgeted gifts. Whenever a new doctoral program is started in a new field—for example, in history—my chief librarian asks for a minimum of $50,000 to be available at the outset to bring library resources up to a starting point, with $10,000 a year for five years over and above the budgeted allocation for library resources. The higher the education, the more varied are the languages, the more specialized the themes, and the more sophisticated the words and ideas. Whether you are reading music or formulae, or logarithms or Spencer or Darwin, one of the functions of a university is to make these forms of accumulated knowledge available and handy. One professor told me that if he could have delivered to his office each day all that was printed in his narrow field, it would be equal to ten sets of encyclopedias per day!

All who face the task of assimilating the vast amount of knowledge now exploding on our modern scene and appearing in a wide variety of media are being helped by the marvels of the computer age. The use of the computer in organizing facts and knowledge of all kinds is one of the exciting frontiers in higher education today. This enormous expanse of knowledge and the increase in the published word in the secular world quadruple our problems and our opportunity. This is particularly true in a church-related university. One of the great responsibilities of a church-related university is its commitment to graduating the humanely educated person. To do this we must be able to include books of scholarly competence dealing with the life and thought of the Christian faith. Finding such books is not easy. We as a church must not leave to the secular publishers the responsibility for publishing the scholarly writings of our great minds in the church. I realize that these books are not always profitable publishing ventures. I wish there were some other way to support the superanuated preachers of the Methodist church so that our publishing house could be freer to lose money on important, urgent publishing responsibilities. This university, if it is to be true to its commitment, must find scholarly books written for the college world, for students and senior scholars, on the life and thought of the Christian faith, both in its history and in its interpretation of our complex contemporary scene. We must be able to turn to the church's publishing arm with equal or perhaps more assurance than to the secular publishers for those books on the life and thought of our faith.

CHAPTER VI

SMU and Public Responsibility

INTRODUCTION

FROM THE HIGH NOON assassination of President John F. Kennedy in Dallas on November 22, 1963, to the lively activities of research and community consciousness raising on civic problems by SMU's new Institute of Urban Studies, the time span seemed long. It was, however, short as universities move. The direction never wavered.

Immediately following the assassination of the nation's young President on the streets of Dallas, the community of Dallas experienced a combination of fear, horror, guilt, and sadness. The city was on the receiving end of massive criticism. Any community which does not reexamine itself when it is on the receiving end of such an onslaught of criticism would appear to be insensitive. Some citizens, however, wanted to put the event away. "This happened *to* us not *by* us," they believed. Others piled onto this event every criticism they held regarding the city's life. Many of these feelings were expressed in the mass media.

President Tate could not accept either of these two viewpoints. In this caldron of anguished emotion, President Tate gave his measured response to the event of November 22 when all around him the expectations were of more emotionalism. President Tate believed that SMU had a special responsibility for its environing community. Toward that end, he took four steps: he convened a university convocation on "A Call to First Principles"; he established a joint SMU-community committee (known as the McFarlin Committee) to explore and propose ways in which there could be better communication between the university and the city on issues of major import; he led SMU in sponsoring, under the leadership of the McFarlin Committee, a series of community-university

85

consultations whose participants included the top leadership and best minds of both the university and the community; and he eventually moved the university into the establishment of the SMU Center for Urban and Environmental Studies, an interdepartmental research facility affiliated with the School of Humanities and Sciences.

Concurrently with the establishment of SMU's Community-University Consultations, the SMU student body under the president of that body, formed the Student Committee on Political Education (SCOPE). They commended the words and actions of the university president and moved into a program to promote a greater understanding of American ideals, principles, and structures in response to the tragedies that had shaken the nation.

A Call to First Principles

During the weekend following the assassination of America's President, and while the nation lived through the televised final tribute to him, the president of Southern Methodist University mourned with the nation and the city and prepared for his meeting with the university community on Tuesday morning, November 26, 1963.

SOUTHERN METHODIST UNIVERSITY, like all mankind, has been grieved and shocked over the assassination of our young president. As a corporate citizen of the Dallas community, the university has shared the grief and responsibility that have been focused on the heart of Dallas. We are deeply saddened. Out of our mourning have come new insights and new motivations. We see more clearly the things we have known, but until this shocking experience have not known well enough.

All great social awareness is born in crisis. As we rise from our knees to join all Dallas citizens, both individual and corporate, what is our task ahead? What do we say? How do we pray? Although mindful of our mistakes and shortcomings, this, now, is no time for continued vindictiveness. It is no time for scapegoating. It is no time for self-abasement and breast-beating. It is a time for reevaluation, for moral and spiritual vitality, and for the rational wisdom that reminds us of those things which are true, eternal, and important for all of us and for our society.

In this spirit, Southern Methodist University, playing its full role as a part of the Dallas community, does now call on the rich intellectual and moral resources of our larger university family, to seek and to articulate a statement of *first principles* for this university and for Dallas of which we are a part. We call our students and our faculty to a fuller commitment to learning in order better to serve their generation. We are confident that all of the agencies of government, the institutions, and the organized groups of Dallas will join in facing their responsibilities with a sense of unity.

Knowing we must reexamine our presuppositions and face not only our past inadequacies but also our potential, this university will call together a series of university commissions to formulate and articulate our first principles in several fields. These working groups of scholars and other members of our university family, joined by leading citizens of the community, will define our opportunities and give us a sense of positive direction to our action, the action that is required of all patriotic Americans as we hallow the name of our martyred President and pledge our allegiance to the new President of the United States of America during these trying days.

These first principles will include:

First: *Our commitment to law and its moral foundations*

There can be no civilized society without law, and no law unless the members of society cherish and uphold it. If we disregard law's proper processes, regardless of the provocation, we undermine civilized society itself. If we dishonor the judges and magistrates who interpret and enforce it, we undermine the foundations of our society. The law that binds us is not merely the law of Dallas, but also the law of Texas, the law of the United States. We are even bound by those humane considerations that bind all nations. We in Dallas are part of a larger community of law, and it is a matter of considerable importance to us and to *all men* that we cherish and uphold our legal obligations in this larger community. If we are to bring integrity to our obligations as citizens, first to this university community and then to our larger community, we must carefully examine all of the evidences of disrespect for the established law of the land.

But legal obligations cannot be fulfilled by adhering to the mere letter of the law. Dedication is also required to the spirit of the law, to those moral foundations of fair and considerate treatment of others, even of those with whom we disagree or whose actions we abhor, upon which all valid law ultimately rests.

Second: *Commitment to community wholeness that values all types of diversity*

Our community lives and grows as it assumes full responsibility for all of the component parts of its life. Every part of our community should be precious to all of us. This university and the city of Dallas have many component parts. Some parts are predominantly racial, some are of national origin. Others are just the normal stratification of any campus or city. Some people are born and raised in one stratum of life and never see another stratum. Other parts of a community are formed around political philosophies. It is a sign of great political maturity when one political group seeks to mirror the wholeness of a community by not turning its back on any segment. It is basic to our political life that we differ and that we disagree. It is basic to our *community life* that we raise our political discourse to this level of maturity. All groupings in our city are important to our life together. But various groupings will *believe* they are an important part of our total life only if they participate in its life fully, as citizens, as workers, as students, as office holders, as church members.

Third: *Commitment to a church that is both independent of its culture and concern to serve it*

I speak as the president of a university with a relationship to a major church body. We have a very close relationship to our sponsoring body. We support and encourage without apology the strong voice of the church, among other voices, on this campus. We honor our role as a university with a theological seminary which trains ministers for the church. We speak, therefore, as a part of the church. If the life of our university community and the community beyond our campus is to reflect the great humane values of our Judeo-Christian tradition, the voice of the church must be heard. It must be heard as an independent, fundamentally free force in the community; it must not merely reflect the values already accepted by the community.

Wherever there is sin and injustice, the church must call us to repentance. Wherever there is hatred, fear, and suspicion, the church must call us to reconciliation. Wherever there is lethargy and disloyalty through indifference to our noble faith, the church must call us to repentance and action. If we, the university, have anything to say to the church at large, let it be said.

Both the church and the university are social institutions, one the family of God in a special way, the other secular. But both are ultimately and fundamentally concerned with the welfare of the individual person, with human dignity and with human fulfillment. Both of these institutions are basic to our society. Both are commissioned to prepare man to live with himself and with his fellow man in peace, security, and fulfillment.

These three areas of commitment are not to be thought of as the limit of our concerns. After further deliberations, we may add additional concerns. These commitments require careful examination. They cannot lie on the table or be placed in a file. They must be examined by this university's community of scholars and community leaders both as to their basic philosophy and as to what specifically they can mean in the day-to-day life of this university and in the larger community beyond our campus.

We have a long-range challenge ahead of us. But it is important to remember that our community needs more than just the negative lament. Our community needs more than just the absence of hate groups. Our community needs the presence of both positive compassion and concern and an enlarging circle of responsible, sensitive intellects. Together, the mind and the compassionate heart represent the basic stature of true humanity. This union, under God, is our greatest source of strength and our most cherished contribution to our civilization. This union of mind and heart, long a major purpose of this university, must find expression in every segment of our society. Each of these segments of society is represented in this university—in law, in teaching, in journalism, in the church, in business, in technology. We have much to learn from each other and much to give to our anguished community.

God bless you, our students. You are our hope for the future. We are especially privileged to have you in our family at this moment in history.

The University and the City

On May 6, 1964, the Southern Methodist University School of Law, in cooperation with the McFarlin Committee, sponsored the first Community-University Consultation between city and university leaders. The subject was "Law: The Supreme Court and the Public Respect for Law." President Tate opened the consultation, giving his studied rationale for the feeding of a vital city-university dialogue on things that matter.

Later in 1964, a second consultation was held on "The Community Responsibility of Church and Synagogue," cosponsored by the Perkins School of Theology and the McFarlin Committee. In 1965, similar conversations were held entitled "A Consultation on Metropolitan Dallas— 1985: The City's Total Living Environment," sponsored by the School of Continuing Education, and a forerunner of the city of Dallas's Goals for Dallas civic study.

The establishment of the SMU Institute of Urban Studies, later to be known as the Center for Urban and Environmental Studies, and still later as Urban Programs of the School of Humanities and Sciences, followed in the later sixties. Each year since has seen a growing number of research projects and community-university consultations on such wide-ranging subjects as "The Economic Potentials in the Goals for Dallas Study"; "Town Lake and Environmental Awareness"; "The Crossroads Community Survey"; "The Alcohol Safety Action Program"—to name only a few.

THIS OCCASION has long been wished for. We find ourselves deeply involved in many things, and do not take the time to sit down with others in our community and discuss serious matters which are of concern to everyone, but about which we do very little face-to-face talking.

It took the assassination of a young President in our city to make us freshly aware of this need for face-to-face communication. We presume that awareness of such a need would come to any city after a tragic event such as we witnessed last November. We speak, however, only for the city we know best, our city. In my convocation address to this university on November 26, 1963, I called for the university to initiate responsible dialogue between its members and leaders from all segments of the community's life. This dialogue must be on matters of important common concern. One of the acute memories of last November is that sense of isolation many of us feel in the midst of our common grief.

There were matters which it seemed to me urgently necessary to discuss. Others seemed to feel the same need. Yet trusted relationships on the level of discussion between the faculty and the town simply did not exist. The established understandings had not been built up. Even well-understood disagreements had not been commonly defined. This community has given to this university a place of honor, and has extended constant and generous support. Members of the university's faculty, individually, play a manifold and many-sided role in the technical, social, cultural, and religious life of the city. But at a moment when as faculty and community leaders we sorely wanted and needed a road to a common forum, we discovered that this road had yet to be built. It is to make a small beginning at developing some significant relationships that the university is initiating these consultations.

While Southern Methodist University is only *one* of the many institutions which are responsible for the public mind and discussion, it nevertheless has a unique role to play, a role which if we fail to fulfill it will simply go by default. That role has to do not only with teaching the future leaders of our society to be competent, compassionate, wise, and courageous; not only with teaching and research and publication carried on with impartiality, discipline, accuracy, and relevance. *The* role which this university *must* play is to be, fundamentally and uniquely, a center of inquiry into the first principles of our common life; to be a clarifier for the individual citizen of what is true, what is just, what is good. The university will accomplish this task not by lecturing *to* the community, but through dialogue *with* the community.

It is against this background that we have invited you to sit down with us today.

CHAPTER VII

Views Expressed to
Special Groups

INTRODUCTION

A LIST of a university president's primary audiences would include such on-campus groups as faculty, students, staff, trustees; and off-campus groups such as parents, alumni, supporters and friends, and business and professional, educational, social, and philanthropic bodies.

This chapter presents President Tate's views expressed to a variety of groups, near and far, over a period of years and covering a number of subjects. The common concern throughout is his desire to interpret Southern Methodist University, its special character and purpose and its special needs, in the larger context of higher education.

The first three selections included in the chapter reflect the developing views of President Tate on the roles of women in higher education and in society. He was no leader likely to move ahead of the culture in enlarging opportunities for women; nevertheless, he became increasingly aware of the role institutions of higher learning must play in preparing young women for what seemed to be less traditionally determined roles for women. President Tate's concept of freedom went beyond youth acting in negation of parental and societal values; he believed that such negation is not freedom. This concept, carried over into the drive for wider life-options for young women, meant to him that their achievement and use of wider life-choices should not duplicate existing evils in society but must enrich all of life.

Three themes run through President Tate's views on women: (1) concern for the enormous waste of intellectual power as women, under social pressures, limit what they will do with their lives; (2) concern that the university help its women students face the barriers that prevent the

92

educated woman from living fully a life she chooses; (3) concern that society, including universities, provide for young women a variety of live *models* from which to choose as they examine the options opening to them in today's world.

The fourth selection is representative of President Tate's words to students. He always welcomed the opportunity to exchange views with each succeeding student generation. While he readily acknowledged that the faculty represented the heart of the university's mission, he loved students and showed infinite patience in listening to them. They refreshed him. They made the burden of his financial efforts on behalf of the university lighter. When he would occasionally "get his back up" in relation to some students, his understanding was enlarged and his anger tempered by student friends from each generation of youth who came to SMU. Keenly aware of the life-style pressures on students, he always tried to offer them alternatives. He wanted a student to feel that it was acceptable to be his own man, her own woman. The early maturation of young people continued to affect the role of the university. In the span of twenty years, universities moved from varying forms of *in loco parentis* in which there were expectations on the part of parents that a college or university would "keep their children safe," to an almost complete abdication of any responsibilities for students, and the assumption, now the law, that all young people are legal adults at eighteen. This change placed unusual stress on a university such as SMU with its concern for a student's total development.

One of the high moments of President Tate's early presidential years was the surprise rally held by the students in the rotunda of Dallas Hall on February 25, 1960. The rotunda and the balconies up to the dome were filled with students as they presented to the president a proclamation expressing "the student body's deep appreciation to him as a man, a citizen and as an educational statesman, their respect for his personal and official integrity, for the atmosphere of free inquiry which he maintains, for his trust in them as students in the conduct of their affairs, and especially for his leadership in guiding SMU in living up to its motto, *Veritas Liberabit Vos*, in full recognition of what he has done to make this true."

The university's trustees formed, of course, another group to whom President Tate had occasion to express his views. In the years following the adoption of the Master Plan, Southern Methodist University's board of trustees moved twice to reorganize the way in which the board was structured. Each change was approved by the South Central Jurisdiction of the United Methodist Church. In 1964, the major changes in the composition of the board included the addition of twenty-five members at large, and stipulations that at least one trustee from each of the states and Annual Conferences of the Methodist Church should be a lay trustee and that trustees should serve three terms of four years each.

A second change was approved in 1968. The board was increased in size to seventy-five elected members, one-half of whom were to be members of the United Methodist Church. Nominations to the board of trustees would now come from the board. Trustees would be nominated from all geographical boundaries of the Annual Conferences of the South Central Jurisdiction but would not be limited to this geographical area. All trustees continued to be elected by the South Central Jurisdictional Conference. All active bishops of the Jurisdiction were members of the board. The orientation and training of this increasing number of trustees became an annual challenge to the president and to the leadership of the board.

Other groups to whom President Tate expressed views represented by selections included here are a graduating class, the faculty, parents, collegiate athletic directors, and alumni gathered at a reunion. Speaking to these varied groups, with their wide range of interests, he served as interpreter of the university and of the purposes of higher education.

A Woman's Choice

Long before the appearance of the various movements concerned with the liberation of women, President Tate was asked by the editors of the Kappa Kappa Gamma magazine, Key, to write an article for them on the emerging concerns about women and higher education. The article, of which we present a shortened version, appeared in the Spring 1960 edition.

IT HAS OFTEN BEEN SAID within recent years that the worst of all twentieth-century irresponsibilities is the dissipation and waste of intellectual potential and talent. If this is true, it is tragic. The gravity of our times requires that we acknowledge it with honesty. Even a casual review of events on the world scene within the last decade gives ample evidence that the last half of the twentieth century will belong to the intellectually strong. This is not an irresponsible generality. It is an onrushing reality.

There is no more searching or difficult problem for a free people than to identify, nurture, and widely use its own talent. This is difficult because a free society cannot commandeer talent. A free society has to be true to its own vision of individual liberty. And yet, at a time when we as a nation face grave and desperate problems, we must see that an undiscovered talent, an undeveloped intellect, a wasted skill, a misapplied ability is a threat to the capacity of a free people to survive.

Those responsible for our colleges and universities today are particularly concerned about the nation's intellectual potential and higher education's role in developing and releasing that potential. Colleges have responded to this in a number of ways. Standards are rising and it is now harder to *get* into most colleges and universities. It is even more difficult to *stay* in. This will increase, not decrease. For those who do receive the green light of admission, the college or university wants only one thing: that each person fulfill his own highest potential. While it may be truthfully said that the greatest dividend on a university's investment in the educational enterprise is a graduate who is capable of responsible, independent thought and action, this is not enough. Such responsible, independent thought and action must reflect a student's *highest* capacity. Otherwise, society's loss is irretrievable.

It is in this context that I introduce the question of women in higher education, women in the arts, the professions, the services which command superior intellectual capacities. In recent years, the experts have trained their sights on women. After woman's political and social emancipation in this country, she has become fair game for the examining eye of the educators, the psychiatrists, the sociologists, the economists, and even the politicians. Her strengths and weaknesses, her intellectual capacities and interests, her influence in the home and community, her political, economic, and legal status have all been examined in detail. Few facts are clearer today than that though women have contributed few great geniuses, they have given consistently to the mainstream of arts, letters, and sciences, and unquestionably have equal capacity with men for high intellectual endeavor. But women have responded neither to the educational opportunities which our society offers to them, nor to the professions, the arts, the sciences which are open to those of superior ability. It is true that more girls go to college than ever before, and that our colleges and universities are equipped to develop their minds toward whatever intellectual goals they might aspire to. Of the students in the highest ten percent of the U.S. high schools who do *not* go to college, however, two-thirds are women. Sixty percent of the girls who are admitted to today's colleges drop out before graduation.

This is a great waste. From the standpoint of our total culture, an equally great loss is to be found in the first-class women mathematicians, the women physicists, the women writers in our college classes, women equal in their capacities to the best men students, who have given no serious thought to the full development of their capacities. These women students, on the whole, plan a life of early marriage with large families. There are those who say that this is fine, that the greatest possible contribution the educated, intellectually superior woman can make is to enrich the lives of her children. There are those who sincerely believe that a mother with unusual abilities and interests in the sciences, in mathematics, or in literature can open doors of immeasurable interest and excitement for her children. With all of this, I must fully agree.

On the other hand, I would like to feel that our young women of superior intellect and ability *have a choice* in the fullest sense of that word; that they are free from the unusual pressures of society, to choose what use to make of their lives. That there are social pressures for early marriage on the American scene today, beginning with the dating mores of earliest adolescence, no knowledgeable person can deny. This kind of subtle pressure is inconsistent with woman's social and political and intellectual emancipation. If there is unusual capacity, it should be socially acceptable, beginning in the home and continuing on the college campus, for a young woman to have intellectual interests.

If there is one thing we need more of it is true intellectuals, whether in the home or in the professions. A true intellectual has an educated mind; she knows that answers to the complex problems of our world must come from rational discussion and thinking. Such a woman does not fall into the traps set for her by persons or groups whose chief stock in trade is manipulation. A truly intellectual woman is receptive to the important values in our American society, and while she is spending her early years at her vocation of homemaking, she can be the bulwark of the intellectual ideal in her club, in the PTA, and in her church.

For the unusually talented young woman who wishes to follow where her talents lead, free from social pressures, into greater specialization, our schools and universities must be less discriminating in giving opportunities for graduate and specialized study. The *Wall Street Journal*, in commenting on Radcliffe's one-year course in business administration for women, believes that in view of the uncertainties ahead for most young women, a one-year program should be a wise investment. Two years and a five-thousand-dollar investment makes sense, however, for the promising young man who knows he is going to spend a lifetime in business. This is a popular approach to the question of women in business, in industry, in the arts and the professions. However, I feel that we need to face some facts of life. A woman faces the possibility of living an average of seventy-two years. Should she follow the current trend of early marriage, she comes to the early age of thirty-three or thirty-four with her last child in school, and with more years ahead of her than she has already lived. What is a woman of unusual intellectual ability going to do with her life from thirty-four to seventy-two years of age? During the years of her college and university life, she must be helped, through various counseling and teaching influences, to take the *long look* at her life. The use she is making of her life fifteen years after graduation is the best test of the depth of her college education. She must be so educated that after fifteen or twenty years she will not wake up a bewildered Rip Van Winkle!

Every effort should be made on our college campuses to keep our superior girls on the campus for four full years. They should be helped to become aware of the grim facts of life: that they will live longer than men, that women are more numerous than men, that women will be widowed too early, that child care will be over and they will be left with forty years to spend, and that it is altogether possible that during their lifetime women may be drafted into the labor force. Whether our young women of superior intellectual ability choose to follow their four years of college with a serious attempt to develop unusual talents in the direction of the arts, letters, sciences, mathematics, or whether they take this up for the last forty years of their life, they represent fully half of our nation's intellectual potential. We cannot afford to lose a single citizen's superior ability![1]

Opening the First Women's Symposium

In the academic year 1965-66, the year of Southern Methodist University's celebration of its Fiftieth Anniversary and the beginning of its second half-century, the first SMU Symposium on the Education of Women for Social and Political Leadership was held. The symposium's original design, continued through the years, called for the exchange of ideas on major issues of the day between women students and interested community women. The participants through the years have come not only from SMU and the Dallas community, but from many colleges and universities and a wide variety of communities.

President Tate opened the first symposium on January 17, 1966.

THIS SYMPOSIUM FULFILLS one of my early hopes for our Fiftieth Anniversary celebrations at Southern Methodist University: that the women of our university community would share significantly in this celebration.

SMU, since its beginning in 1915, has always welcomed women with full equality of academic opportunity. One-half of our present student body are women. This campus would be a dull and far less adequate place to live and work in without you! This symposium makes certain assumptions as it opens. Perhaps the most important assumption is that we are not going to argue the so-called "woman question." We will not argue *whether* women have responsibilities in the world in which they live, but *how* they can best carry out those responsibilities. We are asking three primary questions of every woman in this room: (1) What are the barriers which prevent women from using their potential fully and making their full contribution to the public good? (2) How can these barriers be removed? (3) How can educational institutions and specifically this university move effectively in this process? On these questions we want your best thinking. This is to be a symposium in the truest sense. Every person is a member. We expect you to listen and, most of all, to talk. Your discussion section assignment has been carefully made and you are therefore important to your section.

You are a distinguished, educated group of women. *Why* are you *who you are* today? We need to know your motivation. The number of girls in Texas who go to college and who finish is *far below* the national average. We need the concerned, informed help of such a group as this if we are to see that our society does not lose the educated contribution of a larger percentage of its women. I hope that out of this first Symposium on the Education of Women for Social and Political Leadership may come a continuing group who will help us rethink the education of women for their various roles in the world. This would be a contribution long cherished by this institution as it moves into its second half-century.

Dialogue with the Town Girls of SMU

By 1972, SMU and society in general had moved a considerable distance from the expressed concerns about women of 1960 and 1966. The "women's movement" was in full swing. Young women on campus had had their consciousness raised about life's possibilities for them. The initial study on opportunities opened and those denied to women faculty, students, and staff at SMU had been completed in the academic year 1971-72. The new Commission on the Status of Women at SMU had been appointed by the president in the spring of 1972.

In September, 1972, former President and now Chancellor Tate was invited for dialogue by the Town Girls of SMU. They specifically asked to discuss with him the issue of opportunities for women and SMU. His opening statement to them on September 28 follows.

SOUTHERN METHODIST UNIVERSITY has, for many years, been concerned that doors should be open to women. These doors should be open not so much to change the *image* of woman's role as to *enlarge* it. We need to open up a wider variety of choices of roles for women.

For every choice open to a woman, there should be a live *model* to look at, to question, to listen to. This means that there ought to be not one or two models for your lives as women, but a dozen. As you see these models before you, you must be reassured that whatever choice you make, our culture will find that choice acceptable. There was a time when if you were not engaged by the spring semester of your senior year, it was a catastrophe, especially for your mother! I am all in favor of a fellow picking his girl early, if he wants to and if she wants to! I did! But it ought to be possible for a girl or a fellow to make any one of several choices without society's disapproval.

Most people need *models* in making choices about life-styles and in selecting vocations. For most people, it is hard to become something you have not seen alive and functioning. We have seen women as housewives, teachers, mothers, nurses, secretaries for a long time. Other models are not so easily visualized. Some young women have a rich heritage in *models*. The producer of *Newsroom* on Channel Thirteen is a young professional woman, wife, and mother. She has a long family history of women who have been in the business and professional world. The idea of *models* works for men, also. I remember the first time I saw a man recruited to work in the nursery at my church! Now, this is a common practice. The young women in the Perkins School of Theology, here at SMU, have had a hard time *seeing* their place as professional people in the church. They are surrounded by men. Now, however, the presence of a new faculty member, a woman Old Testament scholar and a Ph.D., will help them *internalize* an option they have been thinking about for their lives.

It is the university's business to see that the *models* for life are not narrow. Without sacrificing quality, and with equal probability of improving quality, we must offer you more options for your life.

In the movement to liberate women, we must not have more women who act like men. "Female masculinity" is no step forward. It is the antithesis of masculine dominance. We must overcome both masculine dominance *and* female masculinity. In the process, we should develop a new and higher understanding of what it means to be a human being. Reducing the "double standard" in sex and moral standards to the lowest level of a common standard gives us no *higher* understanding of human sexuality. Negating the double standard is *not* in itself *a form of liberation*. It is copying the enslavement of some men.

Opening doors of our highly competitive business life to women so that they, too, can die early of heart disease is not *in itself* a form of liberation. We must look for a new level of living, for both men and women. In all of this, women, in their drive for liberation, must help all of us find a new and higher level of *humanness*.

Perhaps I can risk a word or two about men! I really do believe that men have an obsession about masculinity. Their masculinity is easily threatened. In advertising and in the mass media, women are made to think that they are not a success in life unless they are attractive to men. For some women, this is no problem. For others, "attractiveness" must be a many-faceted thing. All of this places a burden on girls and women to be "desirable," and oftentimes at an age when it would be healthier to be less burdened. This media drive for female attractiveness and what girls are led to expect, however, is equally a burden on fellows. They should not always be expected to seduce! We must find a level of relationships and a level of expectations about our humanness where sexuality is not a burden on either the girls or the fellows. Human sexuality is meant to be expressed and enjoyed in many forms and at many levels. Up to now, it is almost impossible for a fellow to have a girl "*chum.*"

Masculinity is also threatened in some kinds of competitive situations. Success and masculinity—authority and masculinity—power and masculinity. All of these are mixed up in our culture. I am not sure what all of this says about the roles of women. Nor do I know how we are going to learn how to deal with many of the threats that seem to be emerging in the new doors that are opening to women. We need your help and your understanding. I welcome your questions and your response to what I have said. I am convinced that we need a great deal more dialogue between girls and fellows about this interesting and important question.

The Role of the Student Leader

The American Association of College Student Unions, Region Twelve, met on the campus of Southern Methodist University on December 11, 1964. The group was composed of elected student leaders from a wide variety of colleges and universities who governed the "Student Unions" or "Student Centers" on their individual college campuses. Following a discussion with them on the changes taking place in higher education in America in the mid-sixties, President Tate suggested four dimensions of student leadership he considered significant.

IN REVIEWING MY YEARS as an undergraduate and graduate student, as dean of students and eventually as president, several important dimensions of student leadership have been impressed upon me.

A student leader must first of all *be a student.* One remark I remember out of the orientation I went through as a freshman in this university was made by a very wise person who said, "Don't miss the main show. Don't get so tied up in the sideshows you never get in the main tent." I think the reason I remembered that so well was that in the little town where I grew up the circus would come to town and have a parade. I would go to see the parade and then think I had seen the circus. It took me a good many years and some growing up to realize that I had missed the main event. You know the booby traps of the willing student leader who will march in every parade, but never get inside the main tent. It is not easy to be both a student and a student leader. Some requirements involved in being a student are hard to work into the role of student leadership. A student must learn to respect the discipline required to search for the truth. A student must learn to be at home in the realm of ideas. A student must also be willing to have his prejudices threatened by discovered truth. This is hard. It is easy to follow clichés and slogans and build up a prejudice rather than examine it. A student must learn to do his own thinking, even when such thinking calls for a student to be a minority and to stand alone.

A second dimension of student leadership *acknowledges the importance of peer group influences*. The greatest learning that can take place in the college community is when the student teaches another student. There is no doubt, I am completely convinced, that learning from one's peer group is probably the most lasting learning. In this process, students confer leadership on their fellow students. To receive this affirmation, a student leader must learn to recognize and tolerate differences. Learning to live and work with differences has to do with the practice of democracy. One of the outstanding features of the student union movement in this country is teaching young people how to work together within the structures of democracy where the concern for the individual is not lost and yet group decisions have to be made. Thus the democratic process can flourish. There isn't a person in this room who wouldn't vote for the democratic process. If, however, you search your heart and analyze your own experiments in manipulation on your own campus, you will find you are giving lip service to democracy! Sometimes you can become autocratic as student leaders by thinking that the end justifies your manipulation and your devious ways of gaining what you think the college or your student union ought to have. It is important at this stage to feel the impact of peer judgments. The democratic process survives on peer influence. The role of the student leader in fostering this kind of healthy influence is essential.

A third dimension of student leadership is the importance of *keeping the administration and the faculty from forgetting you*. There are heightened tensions between the different segments on college campuses today. These tensions are growing. When concern over other issues mounts, it is easier to forget that colleges were created primarily for students! Because of the great demands made upon university officials and faculty members, there is a danger of our becoming indifferent, if not callous, regarding the *sources of discontent* and the *causes of failure* among students. We need your help in remembering *you*!

Students are not called upon, of course, to run the college or university. This is not the role of the Student Union Board or the Student Senate. The responsibility of running the university is delegated and clearly defined in a university's bylaws. It is a mistake when students feel that in the short span of their four-year undergraduate experience they can pick up the reins and run a college or university. You are entitled, however, to know why certain decisions are made. You are entitled to explanations. You are also entitled to a voice that is heard. We have found on this university campus that the judgments of students are helpful and a necessary part of some of the decisions which must be made.

My final word to you is, "Please don't let college life become too grim!" It is true that a college education is serious business and you are going to have to work hard. As leaders of your Student Unions, you are responsible for all kinds of organizations, not the least of which are those concerned with the purely recreational and social aspects of the university campus. It is up to you to see to it that your college campus does not become too tense and too grim. Perhaps the greatest challenge to the Student Union leadership in this particular day is to find a way to create wholesome recreation and good times.

All of us need your refreshing ability to carry both the serious and the fun sides of life with equal aplomb!

A Working Partnership:
The University and Its Trustees

In the spring of 1968, a large group of new trustees was elected to SMU's board of trustees. At the conclusion of their orientation, training

and committee assignments, the new trustees met with President Tate
on November 7, 1968, prior to the fall meeting of the board of trustees.
He expressed to them his dependence upon them and the hope which
their presence brought to SMU.

I WELCOME YOU HERE to share the responsibilities I carry for this university. The longer I work in higher education, the more I am convinced
that no person ought to meddle with universities who does not *know*
them well, and still *love* them. Knowing and *still* loving is one of life's
greatest challenges. A university president must not only love youth and
scholarship. He must cheerfully and aptly raise millions of dollars, supervise hundreds of faculty and staff members, and oversee complex research activities. In uniquely personal ways, he can sharply influence the
education of a generation that is preparing to live in an age of great
change. This is an awesome power and a great obligation.

This enormous job would not be possible for any president if he
were not backed and supported by an informed and loyal board of trustees. The American system of college and university governance is unique.
I have never been able to discover why the founders of Harvard College
chose to follow a model quite different from that which they knew, the
model of Oxford and Cambridge. However, they did. They created the
concept of the lay board of trustees. American colleges and universities,
from that day forward, have followed Harvard's lead. We call this group
by different names: Overseers, regents, trustees. They are all groups of
noneducators responsible for the essential policies of our higher educational system.

You, the trustees of Southern Methodist University, have this demanding job. Beginning now, you are *not* visitors to this campus. You
are integral parts of this university. We could not continue to exist and
function without you or someone like you.

I assume your commitment. Let me now define what I think that
means. You do have a commitment to the university as a whole. It is
urgently important for you to know this university's founding purposes
and its present overall goals. It is important, however, for each of you
to pick your spot of special interest. You will be sensitive to the particular
needs of the university which you discover through your special interests.
Your committee assignment is designed to help you choose and serve
well some special part of this university. We will need your specialized
interpretation. When the board of trustees is together as a board, how-

ever, you will need to be aware that your specialized interests stand alongside many other interests, because SMU has many diverse parts: the arts, technology, liberal learning, professional schools in various fields, libraries, student life. Decisions are made upon the basis of what is good for the whole.

The president is your representative to the faculty, the staff, the students. The president is their representative to you. This is important to the solid administration of any university. It is important *to me* that the trustees of SMU understand this. I do not want to appeal for your sympathy, but I do want your understanding of the many facets which make up the community known as SMU. It is no easy job to keep this big, expensive, sensitive, dynamic organism going on the right track. I don't very often like to share letters I get. Some of them should not be read in public. Some, however, are very much worth sharing. Last week I received a letter from one of our fine senior girls. She sent me a quotation which she hoped would help me in what she called my conscientious struggle to be all that my demanding office requires. Then she closed the letter by asking about the president. Who is he, she asked. Then as if to answer her own question she said that the president is a daring pioneer who fills an impossible post. I may not be all of that, but it helps to have someone say it!

Not only is it important to *me* that you understand how we work, but it is also important to *you* to know how we work. You can be subject to pressure if we allow it. We believe that you must have intimate knowledge, the best briefings possible. You are then free to set policies for SMU, as directed by the bylaws of the university. Your committee work can give you many opportunities for gaining deep insight into the workings of our schools and our campus life. There are some things, however, that trustees *never* do. You never ask for football tickets! You do not get into the admissions business! You write letters of recommendation, yes. Pressure, no! Do not be dismayed if you hear speeches with which you do not agree. A university cannot and should not be engaged in thought or speech control.

I go into this period of the restructuring of our board of trustees with a great deal of optimism. Someone has said that optimism is the range finder of the future. Higher education, and particularly private higher education, needs range finders of the future. Trustees become statesmen only as they comprehend the meaning of higher education and work vigorously to defend it. We all know that in today's fast-changing technological society the roles of a university are many. A university plays a pivotal role in shaping the human spirit. A university campus must provide hospitable shelter for students to think things over, with some margin of time given to dreaming.

Trustees must recognize that the college or university is not only a place where past achievements of the race are preserved and transmitted, but also a place where the conventional wisdom of the present day is constantly subjected to merciless scrutiny. A trustee who accepts this fact will remain poised when surrounded by crosscurrents of controversy. He will understand that tension and abrasion are inevitably present wherever the search for truth is being honestly conducted. He knows that in any university worth its salt there will be, in Milton's words, "much arguing, much writing, many opinions, for opinions in good men are but knowledge in the making." A trustee will come to view friction as an essential ingredient in the life of a university, and vigorous debate as a sign not of decadence, but of robust health.

All of this requires a sophistication rooted in wisdom and a wisdom which encompasses not just a single institution, but the entire world of higher learning. Therefore your service on this board of trustees serves all institutions of higher learning, and in a peculiar and special way it serves Southern Methodist University. You represent a considerable *lift* in my hope for the future of this university. Someone has said that *hope* is the source of energies for new options. We have had a vigorous past. As Churchill once said, "We haven't come this far because we're made of sugar candy!" We need your energies, now, for our future. We welcome you. We intend to count on you.

What Have You Done with My Life?

During the nineteen commencement exercises in which President Tate participated, those of 1954 to 1972, he followed the example of President Umphrey Lee in giving a very brief message to the graduating students. His statement at the commencement of 1968 is presented here because it sums up, at a particularly difficult time, what the president thought a college education at Southern Methodist University should mean to the graduates.

Commencement 1968 brought to a close the second of what were to be hard years of student unrest. The late winter of 1968 had seen the end of draft deferment for graduate students; the Columbia University violence had just ended; the SMU campus had experienced a year of non-violent but continuous controversies reflecting the tensions of the times. President Tate joined in spirit hundreds of other college and university presidents who pondered the question of what to say to graduates in that spring of 1968.

WE COME TO A COMMENCEMENT DAY in higher education in America today with a question mark hanging over a growing number of institutions of higher learning. Students, faculty, administrators, trustees, alumni, the general public are asking searching questions of our universities, *big* questions about nature and role; *deep* questions about purpose and about goals.

I hear another question. It is a little question spoken sometimes softly, sometimes so softly it is not heard at all except by the person asking it. This is the question in the mind of the *graduate*: "What have you done with *my* life?" You have a right to ask that question. You have a right to expect that your university has invited you, has intrigued you, yes, has pushed you into knowing something positive about life. Here on this campus you have been exposed to great minds, wonderful books, beautiful art. What is it you should have learned here?

We hope you have learned that *life is a celebration,* not a lament; that life is good and meant to be lived, not denied, both for you and for all persons. *Cynicism is not becoming* to a university community or to its members. If this university has brought you to this commencement day knowing that life is a celebration, this is, indeed, a great day.

If you come to this day equipped to face life positively, you can be grateful. The values you brought to this campus have no doubt changed during your years here. I remember the traumatic adjustment of my own adolescent sense of right and wrong, good and bad, important and trivial, beautiful and ugly, worthy and worthless. Looking back, I now realize it was this refinement of my values that was the important product of my college life. The maturity, the growth that came to my life commitments during my college years was the real stuff that made commencement day one to remember.

For this day to be a celebration for *this university*, as well as for you, we must believe that the many influences of the university have made their mark on you. Let me suggest three marks of maturity we hope are present now in your life as a direct result of your education at this university.

First, we hope you are a person whose judgments and important decisions are enormously influenced by your ability and your willingness to think. To know and to recognize facts, to be acquainted with authorities, either personally or by their writings, to have access to computer and library services is important, but this is not enough. The educated person must be able and willing to think. He must be willing to bring his ability to reason to all the problems which confront him and his world. We live in a day when contagious hysteria and social pressures can completely anesthetize a person's power to reason. In such a state of numbness, a person finds it hard to spot the phony, to recognize the hypocritical, to isolate the demigod. Emotion is an essential part of the will to act. But emotion can never take the place of rational judgment. The emotional outburst, whether engaged in by an individual or a group, is adolescent and anti-intellectual and anti-university. It is the profound hope of this university that its graduates are persons whose response to problems, difficulties, conflicts is the response of the thinking person.

Second, we hope that you are committed to human values over material values. This is a hard commitment to live up to. This university, which hopes it has taught you this discernment of value, has to fight every day of its life to be true to such a commitment. There is a rhetoric gap between oratory and reality in higher education. There is some of that gap here at this university. We do firmly reassert, however, that at this university people *are* more important than things. To build a faculty *is* more important than brick and mortar. We are encouraged in this commitment by growing signs among our students that they are no longer "hung up" on material security. We hear them say that people are more important than fiscal assets, that ideas outrank things, and that love is the *only* lasting value. To spell out what these statements mean in the world of business, government, education, homemaking—this is your challenge today.

Third, we hope that you have found here or have had refined here *a faith to live by*. If you have no faith to live by, your life lacks a dynamic center. God, by whatever name you choose to use, represents that which is ultimate for you, that which demands your highest loyalty. What voice do you hear today *above all others*? We have failed you here at SMU if we have given you knowledge and let your soul wither. Mankind's past experiences and his search for meaning fill our libraries and our art galleries. Our university community has within it people whose faith is deep-rooted and relevant to life today. You have had opportunities to be directly involved in the anguish and the aspirations of other people, many less fortunate than you. I hope that in the course of this intellectual and spiritual pilgrimage you have found time-tested, eternal values to live by.

In times of rapid change, the *old* may be destroyed along with the *decayed*. There *are* some time-tested, eternal values. Each generation must be responsible for the validation of the true and the throwing off of the false. There is an illustration taken from an ancient book which has always said something to me. It is the story of a man who turned out to be foolish about the place he picked to build his house on. What makes him foolish is that he didn't know the difference between sand and rock. Perhaps you will recall the verse, ". . . . a wise man builds his house on a rock. The foolish man builds his house on the sand . . and is not prepared for the storms. . . ."[2]

One thing I can promise you is storms.

If the diploma I give to you today is a symbol of your ability and willingness to reason, of your commitment to human values over material values, and if this diploma is a symbol of the fact that you have found a faith to live by, then this university is fulfilled in you, and society will be blessed through your life in the years to come.

Higher Education's Paradox

President Tate's relationship to the general faculty, as a body, was never without the normal faculty-administration tensions. He was at the same time their chief advocate and their chief adversary. The medieval oath which the dukes and the squires of Aragon took to the king of Aragon could describe the "conditionals" which governed the faculty's relationship to the university's president:

> *We who are as good as you, swear to you who are not*
> *better than we,*
> *to accept you as our king and sovereign lord, provided*

that you
observe all our liberties and powers;
but if not, then not.[3]

Even so, President Tate never hesitated to level with the faculty about any issue of major concern to him involving higher education in general and Southern Methodist University in particular.

In his annual statement to the general faculty on September 1, 1970, President Tate felt it was urgent to remind the faculty of the need for public assurance of the validity of higher education and of a university's ability to manage its own affairs. The bombing of the University of Wisconsin's Army Mathematics Research Center on August 25, 1970, climaxed a year of violence and disruptions on college campuses. The public needed to know that leaders of America's institutions of higher learning were capable of exercising their responsibilities with care and competence. President Tate knew that Southern Methodist University needed the support of all segments of the university, including in a special way the general faculty.

OUR COLLEGES AND UNIVERSITIES face a paradox. The more responsive the public has been in providing educational opportunities, the more the universities seem to be threatened by hostile forces and instability within their own house. For many years there has been a growing attack upon higher education. On the whole, universities were caught off balance. We have not known how to defend ourselves. This is an unfortunate state for an enterprise growing as fast as higher education is growing. The college population has tripled during the last twenty years. During the last decade numbers increased from over three million to seven million. This has meant that new colleges have been opened at the rate of almost one per week. Between 1957 and 1967 as much college and university capacity was added to this country's educational resources as had been provided in the previous three hundred years.

Yet such growth and expansion has not come without its problems unique to our day. Of all the crises in higher education that have been identified, perhaps none is more important than the *new skepticism* that denies the possibility of objective, rational thought. Either we are able to meet this kind of skepticism, or we are out of business as a university and are only running a trade school.

To meet this kind of challenge, we must count on the most serious commitment of educators. By educators I do *not* mean university presidents who speak generically about universities; neither do I mean the large bureaucratic philanthropies who influence higher education. I mean the educator who meets his classes, seminars, preceptorials, laboratories every week. The faculty member is the *key* to any challenge which has been leveled at higher education and its relevance for today's world. Our strength at Southern Methodist University has always been in our great teachers, as those of us who are alumni can attest. Our weakness is in the careless, indifferent, and ineffective teaching on the part of a few. In too many instances, the cynicism of students has stemmed from unchallenging and sorry experiences in the classroom or laboratory. It is the faculty's responsibility to know about any sorry academic performance of its members and to judge them. There is a great tradition and a discipline within the profession of the educator. In the June 1970 issue of the *Journal of the American Association of University Professors* there is an article which calls professors to uphold certain standards of professional responsibility. Chief among those listed is the duty and the willingness of faculty members to *make professional judgments upon each other.* This must mean a more careful evaluation of teachers by their peers; it also means involving students in some form of judgment of those who teach them.

I want to commend publicly four of our schools for the programs of faculty evaluation now being carried on, all of which have some degree of student evaluation of those who teach them. While I want to encourage this developing process of evaluation, let me say very frankly that the most important judgment passed upon those who teach must be the judgment of their peers. The real meaning of academic freedom is twofold. A faculty member is free to search for the truth and to teach that portion of the truth as he knows it. But the faculty is also responsible for sitting in judgment upon peers as they exercise their freedom. The American Association of University Professors is eminently right in calling the faculty to that professional responsibility.

This year must also be a year when we say less about innovating programs in our catalogues, but *see* more faculty members relating personally to students in class and out of class. Catalogue statements do not create a climate. Presidents' speeches do not create a climate. Teachers who care about young people, teachers who give more than the time of day to their students, teachers who really turn students on intellectually, *do* create a climate. Out of this relationship will come all of the innovations in program this university could possibly want. The faculty of Southern Methodist University represents our greatest hope and our first line of defense against the rising tide of skepticism in this country concerning the worth of one of this nation's noblest institutions, its universities.

Don't Send Your Child to a University!

Throughout the years of his presidency, President Tate always considered groups of parents to be one of his major communication responsibilities. He met annually with various groups of parents: the SMU Mothers Club, the Dads Club, the parents of entering students, and alumni groups. In addition to discussing with them the state of the university, he shared with them his knowledge of the forces in society and on the college campus affecting the lives of students. One of his constant concerns was that parental expectations regarding the university's responsibility for its students would extend to in loco parentis, *a concept fast disappearing, if it ever really existed, on college campuses.*

By 1971 the hard years of student unrest of the sixties were over. The president of Southern Methodist University was emotionally drained. He was now president of a university where a youth of eighteen years was a legal adult. The president felt that he had to help parents understand that a university campus was no place for a child. The group to which this statement was made was composed of members of the Methodist Men's Club and guests of Dallas's Highland Park United Methodist Church, meeting on March 15, 1971.

WHEN I SPEAK to a group of parents—and grandparents—I assume your concern for young people. I assume your deep interest in the forces which influence the lives of our young who are now adults at eighteen.

Don't send your *child* . . .

We are all fully aware of the stages of development in life. A child's life is one continuous series of experiences involving care, new experiences, freedom, discipline, love, and growth. If any of these are left out or neglected, his life is deprived. An adolescent, in the understanding which our society, our culture, gives, is something we call part-child and part-adult. When do you say of your son or daughter: He or she is no longer a child? When they are able to earn their way? When they are sexually mature? When they no longer seek your advice and help? When they can vote? For the young men, when they are drafted?

Parents often believe their son or daughter is still a child when parents pay the bills; when the son or daughter still keeps the home address; when a son or daughter makes a mistake in judgment or makes a different judgment than the parents would make. Each of us probably has a rather mixed-up concept of when childhood ends and adulthood begins.

Society has had changing ways of conferring adulthood. In primitive cultures, we have learned of the adolescent initiation rites, the ceremonies of passage from childhood to adulthood. Even in the early years of this Republic, because of the nature of work, a youth could be accepted as man or a woman when he or she was able to do a man's or a woman's work.

Now, however, the situation is different. Here and in most of the Western world, our society tends to regard a youth as no longer a child but not yet an adult. Our technological development has added to this *dependency* role of youth. Today it is difficult to move into a productive role in society and be financially independent without more education and training than earlier generations had to have. As a result, we have young men and young women twenty-one, twenty-two, twenty-three, and even twenty-four years old still financially dependent upon their parents.

Behavioral scientists will tell you that in our culture we have lowered the age of puberty by two and a half years. At the same time, we have increased the years of economic dependency by from five to eight years. This sets up an inevitable tension between our young people and those in the adult world.

Our sons and daughters know a great deal about our world. They have grown up in our mass culture. A continuous part of their expanding awareness of their worlds has come through the mass media, especially television. They have also grown through travel. Young people are traveling this world over to an extent beyond the imagination of most of us when we were young. With this expanding awareness has come not only more knowledge, but a questioning. With more learning, they now have a "conscience of knowledge."

Many young people today do not share our social and political viewpoints. Many young people question our values. In varying degrees, our young are moving to form their own value systems. They want to find out about life and about our ways of socially organizing ourselves *for themselves!* Some are expressing these values in their own subculture. A fifteen-year-old boy may still live in your home, but when such rock songs as "Healin' River" and "I Don't Know How to Love Him" from the rock opera *Jesus Christ, Super Star* are literally worn out being played on his stereo, you know that we have a generation of youth who will not continue to fit into the molds of our present adult society without serious questioning on their part. In some cases, we will experience outright rejection.

Some youth seriously question. Some youth flippantly question. Some youth just "cop out" because of either deep alienation or a difference in values so wide they seem unable to cope. For some, the strain between maturity and economic dependency is simply too great. On the other side of this coin, our same society declares a young Marine an adult when he has finished boot camp. There is no preferential treatment. There are no protections normally reserved for "a child." In this complex, confusing transition from childhood to adulthood in our culture, how do our youth go about declaring their adulthood? They can marry. They can become parents. They can become Marines. They can finish school and work. They can quit school and work. They can cop out.

The university is caught in the middle of this "child" versus "adult" controversy. A university is *not* a baby-sitting institution. If you send a child to a university, he or she will get hurt. A university is one of the institutions of our society with particular responsibility for training the mind, for structuring ways in which young people can gain knowledge, and then it is to be hoped there will develop some *conscience of knowledge* which will send graduates out into our society equipped to provide the precise tools for society's growth and change, all for a better, a happier, a more peaceful world.

I must also say to you, "Don't send *your* child . . ."

One of the best quotations I have ever read on this subject is from *The Prophet* by Gibran:

> And a woman who held a babe against her bosom said, Speak to us of children.
> And he said:
> Your children are not your children.
> They are the sons and daughters of Life's longing for itself.[4]

The writer continues, describing the parent as the bow, the child as the arrow:

For even as He loves the arrow that flies, so He loves also the bow that is stable.

Sooner or later, the bow must let go and the arrow is on its way! Turn loose!

Finally, in today's world, no parent *sends*. No son or daughter can be *sent* to a college or university. Changes in admissions standards and the increase in the number of applicants for admission have alerted our young people from early high school years to apply to several colleges with a willingness on the part of both parents and youth to go where accepted. We are also facing the fact that a youth need not go to college directly from high school. Young people are considering the possibility that a year or two working may be a wise investment of time and energy. In the midst of these changing conditions, we now do not *send* our youth. As a matter of fact, we are all learning that we cannot *send* them anywhere!

Our sons and daughters, if they choose to come to a university, must enter with a good understanding of its meaning for their lives, its potential value for them, its possible hazards and its possible rewards.

Don't *send your child* to a university!

To Collegiate Athletic Directors

President Tate was an All–Southwest Conference player and nominated All-American in football during his undergraduate years at Southern Methodist University. He later became a member of the National Football Foundation and Hall of Fame. His interest in and support of college football never wavered. Until the day of his retirement, he looked as if he could still hold his own in the line.

In the ups and downs of intercollegiate football during his presidency of SMU, there were people who asked, "Is President Tate a football president?" Not so, say those who had to work under his critical eye.

President Tate knew that a university could survive quite well without football, and he said so many times. Football, on the other hand, could not survive without the college campus. Perhaps no one knew better than he the need for crucial reforms in this sport.

On June 21, 1971, President Tate gave his views, excerpted here, on the need for reform in intercollegiate football at the annual meeting of the Collegiate Athletic Directors in Miami Beach, Florida.

I AM GOING TO TALK TO YOU very bluntly about the life and tenure of your profession, because I think your profession is dying. I want you to tell me what you plan to change to. I don't know whether you are going to teach Latin at your university or college or try out for librarian, or whether you are going to be a computer programmer. We are getting quite a few openings in computer programming now. Or maybe if you are really hard up you might be talked into being president. I want to make it very clear that I think the intercollegiate athletic program in this country is running on a suicide course, and the purpose of my being this frank with you is that I am hoping to jar you enough, to make it personal enough, to make you get so mad at me you will go into your discussion groups and talk about it a little. I know I am going to be the fall guy in this and will never be invited back, because I really intend to make you sore today.

Not only is your job in jeopardy, but while all of this is going on, the athletic directors and coaches are playing the game just as if it were not so. If I have a third point, it's this: it's late.

Before I begin to enumerate some of my contentions, I want to assure you that I am not one who is antagonistic to intercollegiate athletics. I am a strong supporter of intercollegiate athletics, both locally in the home situation and across the country. I am a product of intercollegiate athletics. A great many of the values that I feel should be maintained come from intercollegiate athletics. I promote them wherever I can. If this were not so, I wouldn't be here today.

I also want to say I am not sore at my athletic director. This isn't something that is personal. I am not mad at him or the local administration. I am talking, however, about national intercollegiate athletics in this country. There are many factors that threaten the life of intercollegiate athletics, and almost all of them are related to *change*. Intercollegiate athletic programs are no longer the chief spectator sports in the United States. The pros have taken over, and the pros are a lot smarter than we are. I understand you had some discussion this morning about how much smarter the pros are about merchandising and promoting and glamorizing their product. We are no longer the chief topic of conversation of adolescent or high school boys and girls. No longer does the alumni and student support of any college or university depend upon the health of the intercollegiate athletic program.

No longer can the intercollegiate athletic department maintain that it is different from the rest of the university in influence, in priority and function, and in the way it handles its students, the way it recruits its students, and the way it lives. It can no longer justify this type and kind of connection with intercollegiate athletics. No longer will national prestige depend upon football rating. No longer will race be exploited as we have seen it exploited in intercollegiate athletics. I have a special talk on that particular subject. Let me say right now that we have not solved that problem yet.

All of these are very important changes that should alarm you if you don't want to become a computer programmer. The biggest factor, however, in all of these concerns is the financial problem. It is a very simple crisis. Our costs are going up at a very rapid rate, and our income level is falling. We see no optimistic way to solve our problems with more income. There are no men to pay the bills or underwrite the needless deficits. There is no way to find some smart salesmanship in order to get somebody to share tuition costs with the intercollegiate athletic program.

What you need to know and remember is that this is a time of crisis in *all* academe. Every part of every university is having a tough time. I heard the other day that three-fourths of the private institutions in this country are operating on a deficit. Things are beginning to get rough, and you have to realize that this is a different ballgame than you have ever had before. Already we see signs, where we find curtailment of minor sports. We see some very fine traditional intercollegiate athletic programs beginning to wither up and withdraw from competition. Yet it seems to me that the coaches—I am speaking generally—and some of the athletic directors are the last to realize that we have a very severe fiscal crisis.

I know there is great variety in kind and size of athletic programs in this country. It is hard to generalize. I do know, however, that there are big-time athletic departments who cannot pay for their own activities, and who must abdicate the independence of control they have had. When they do, I think they will abdicate their survival. They do not all use the same format, I realize, and some colleges are long in tuition money to support the athletic program.

There are, however, a couple of optimistic notes. The first is that the rising costs are the result of our own doing, rather than some vague hurricane or something that hit us. We made the fiscal costs. This being true, perhaps we can be smart enough and come to our senses soon enough to deal with rising costs—costs our competition has forced us into. In my conference, the Southwest Conference, it is possible to take fifty freshmen athletes a year on full athletic scholarship in football. I don't believe there is anybody here who can make a good case that you could *ever* possibly use fifty freshmen a year in intercollegiate football. In our university, each one costs us about $3,000 a year, so if we ever get fifty (we never did get fifty; forty-eight, I think was the most) that would be a $600,000 commitment in four-year football scholarships for our university that we would make with every incoming freshman class. We hear that the pros are smart. You know, they are smarter than *that*. They do not spend money that wildly. We hear stories about their giving a lot of money away, but they really wouldn't quite do that! They wouldn't do that because they don't need that many players! How many do they have, forty-five? I know you have freshmen standing around for a year without using them. I didn't mean to get that particular about your problem, but I am just trying to show you how we have to take forty-eight players (if we can get them) because Arkansas takes forty-nine!

The same thing is true with the number of coaches. I was surprised to hear that a good many universities have more coaches in sports than the professionals have. I heard one time in a committee meeting that there was one school that had fifteen coaches—football coaches! Maybe we need that many if we are going to give fifty scholarships. This is pretty expensive. Of course, the reason we have to have so many coaches is that our competition does. We raise each other, by this internal competition. If they do it, then we have to do it.

If we lose control in some of the decisions and competitions, *it is our own doing*. Maybe we will get smart enough to come to grips with it.

I am also optimistic over finding that the NCAA committee dealing with this matter is a very, very serious committee. This committee has worked long and hard to come to some solutions of these problems and these necessary controls. I firmly believe controls must be found on the *national* level. I did not always believe that. I thought our conference could put its head together and pretty well decide what we wanted to do and let the rest of the world decide what it wanted to do. I have always been a state's rights man. These problems, however, have to be controlled on the national level. We have independents all around us and other conferences who are competing with us. Individual conferences cannot handle these problems. I think it is harder to enforce and supervise nationally, but I think we are there.

We *do* have a financial crisis in intercollegiate athletics today. It is serious enough to kill off intercollegiate athletics in the near future unless we come up with the answers. It *is* later than it has ever been before.

Looking Back

After becoming chancellor, President Tate was asked to look back over the years of his presidency and share with the Alumni Association Reunion on October 28, 1972, his thoughts on the important things that had happened to SMU during those years.

A LONGER PERIOD OF REFLECTION may change this list, but as I look back now, it seems to me that the most important things that have happened to SMU since the mid-fifties are:

First: The process which the university as a whole went through to create *The Master Plan* in 1962-63. The depth of thinking and searching, the crosscurrents of opinions, the true dedication among all segments of SMU to doing the job well, made the period of "master planning" a turning point in SMU's history.

Second: The growth and development of our fine professional schools, particularly during the sixties, and the decision to offer the Doctor of Philosophy degree in carefully selected areas, with appropriate library growth, have really made SMU a *uni*versity.

Third: The creation of the University College, with its liberal learning core in the curriculum of all who receive a baccalaureate degree from SMU. We meant it when we said that every baccalaureate degree recipient from SMU must be "educated both to live and to make a living."

Fourth: The creation of the School of the Arts and its endowment by Algur Meadows. There are those who shuddered at the idea of putting all the arts together under one roof! We have done it, and have come up with one of the finest faculties and administrations in the country. Their work separately and together is nothing short of stunning.

Fifth: The Master of Liberal Learning Program, which offers the Master of Liberal Arts (MLA) degree. This is a continuing education program whose success can only be measured by the massive response of the public to its offerings. People with degrees in all kinds of fields and at all stages of their lives are coming back to take a degree in liberal learning at the Masters level.

Sixth: The selection of faculty from the pool of young Ph.D. graduates and younger teachers and researchers is now clearly *a choice* for SMU. Any graduate of a first class university is happy to consider SMU among the top choices, as he or she seeks a position.

Seventh: Selective admissions, open to all who wish to apply, have brought us the finest caliber of students we have ever known on this campus. They come from all over the nation. This has made SMU a national institution. We have not accepted selective admissions as a lockstep process, but have been humane and innovative. We are learning better each year how to judge whether a student can benefit from the educational opportunity which SMU offers.

Eighth: SMU can now face passionate differences and controversy without disruption. We have never had disruption. We have both the university-wide structure to deal with disruption and the mind and heart-set to use that structure.

Ninth: SMU is comfortable with the assurance that *openness* is more valuable than dogma. Dogma can be spoken and defended. It can also be challenged.

Tenth: In the years since the fifties, we have completed one of the finest physical plants in the United States. We still have a few spots that need attention. The renewal of old buildings remains a constant need, of course.

Eleventh: The recruitment of friends and supporters for SMU through the years has made the difference between mediocrity and a first-class education for our youth. The $3,300,000 in annual gifts to the budget spells that difference.

Twelfth: There is a sense of community involvement and trust in all major all-university affairs. This is a source of genuine strength. The maintaining of institutional unity through years of growth and testing of power cannot be accomplished by a president alone. It is an institutional achievement, and all share in its success.

CHAPTER VIII

Securing SMU's Financial Future

INTRODUCTION

FROM THE ADOPTION of SMU's Master Plan with its cost requirements in May, 1963, to the formal launching of the $159 million Program of Advancement in January, 1970, Southern Methodist University's major development and funding effort experienced an up-and-down history. The "ups" were encouraging. Assets of the university increased from $70,621,628 in 1965 to $130,272,538 in 1969. The endowment grew from $16,972,827 in 1965 to $26,085,788 in 1969. The annual university budget increased from $11,815,899 in 1965 to $25,503,537 in 1969. The full-time faculty grew from 287 in 1965 to 502 in 1969. During the sixties campus buildings increased by fourteen, including the Owen Arts Center of ten units.

The years of the middle and later sixties were filled with many concerns, not the least of which were the major studies of SMU's potential. The Ford Foundation study of the mid-sixties, with its five years of history and its ten years of projections in anticipation of a major Ford Foundation grant, was an all-consuming effort. (The grant never came; SMU reached its projections without the grant.) The equally exhaustive study of SMU's capabilities for meeting its share of the responsibility of the state of Texas for the higher education of its youth was completed in the late sixties and became a part of the total contribution of privately governed colleges and universities, as requested by the Texas legislature.

Southern Methodist University, however, was yet to launch a major funding program in support of its own future. Planning, however continuous, is in danger of being thought of as improvisation unless accompanied by a major funding program commensurate wth a university's educational aspirations. Efforts to launch such a drive were continuous. On April 3, 1964, the board of trustees authorized a John Price Jones study of needs and potential for funding SMU's Master Plan and the future. The report was received by the trustees in November, 1964; the trustees authorized the drafting of plans for a major funding campaign. In November, 1965, the plans were accepted and funding goals approved.

During this period, the board of trustees was enlarged twice, first in 1964 and later in 1968.

The Southern Association of Colleges and Schools, SMU's accrediting body, had made its regular ten-year visit and review of SMU in the academic year 1963-64. Because SMU had made several major academic structural changes in the Master Plan, the Southern Association requested a five-year return visit in 1968-69. In preparation for this visit, SMU's Self-Study Committee worked for eighteen months in 1967-68 and 1968-69. Out of its labors came a twelve-part report submitted to the Southern Association's visiting team of twenty educators.

Part Twelve of the Self-Study dealt with SMU's plans for the future. Using this document, plus the highlights of the visiting team's report, the University Planning Council of SMU prepared for the May meeting of the board of trustees in 1969 the proposal, "The Issue and the Opportunity," a careful look at SMU's urgent needs for the next five years. This report was accepted and adopted by the board of trustees at that meeting.

From 1966 to 1969, President Tate sought, found, and lost three vice presidents for development. The last of the three development executives came to SMU in September, 1969, but died of a heart attack on November 8, seven days before the fall meeting of the board of trustees. President Tate knew the momentum of the late sixties must not be lost. On November 11, 1969, he called on Dean Joseph D. Quillian, Jr., of the Perkins School of Theology, to become the interim executive for development. At its November 14, 1969, meeting, the board of trustees gave its full support to an immediate implementation of a major funding campaign, and approved a proposal for a called meeting of the board on January 8, 1970, to launch the campaign. Under the excellent leadership of Dean Quillian, assisted by Larry Ter Molen—who later became vice president for development—the funding campaign was ready to be launched on January 8, 1970. The goal was $159 million dollars.

The Issue and the Opportunity

On January 8, 1969, the Bob Hope Theatre was filled with trustees and other university representatives. On the big screen had just been shown a filmed conversation between President Tate and Father Hesburgh, president of Notre Dame University, on the role and opportunity in America today of privately governed institutions of higher learning.

Under the chairmanship of Bishop Kenneth Pope, the board of trustees heard trustees Ross L. Malone, James F. Chambers, Bishop O. Eugene Slater, William P. Clements, Jr.; faculty representative Professor Sydney Reagan; and Student Body President Lon Williams speak on the opportunity now facing SMU and especially its board of trustees.

President Tate then rose to speak, giving personal leadership to this $159 million campaign.

TODAY THE LEADERSHIP of this board of trustees is proposing to the board that Southern Methodist University launch immediately a $159 million dollar Program of Advancement.

I have decided that, rather than give you a formal address, I will share with you some of the trauma of trying to lead this university toward a decision about what we will be doing in the decade of the seventies; what we hope to accomplish; what we will gain; how we will pull it off. These are hard questions. They disturb me. They disturb the university. We are waiting today for your decision. Any design for the future is temporary until this board has the chance to examine it, change it, comment on it, and finally adopt it for action.

Another year could be spent in refining the goals of this Program of Advancement, giving us more time to be more sure of every detail of the program. However, if we were to put the Program of Advancement off another year, even to get better prepared, we just never would make it. We cannot wait. Neither can we fail! Every part of this program is essential to this university's future.

The primary point I want to make with you this morning is that we can seek money for this Program of Advancement with genuine confidence. We can do this because we have a good institution to sell. Many years ago, J. J. Perkins taught me my first lesson about raising money. I was a very young man, an elementary school principal in San Antonio and a recently elected member of the board of the Methodist Home in Waco. I assure you I was the junior member of that board. I used to come to the board meetings and sit and listen to Mr. Perkins, Mr. Bridwell, and other great Methodists, who were giving leadership to that institution. I learned a lot. I remember one time Mr. Perkins told me how hard it was to give money away. This was amazing to me. Here was a man who had money, and he said that it was hard to give money away! He went on to say that the funny thing about giving away money to institutions is that those who need it *most* are the *least* good risks and that when you try to salvage a weak institution by giving it another chance before it goes under, it is not a very good investment. He got around to saying that really the best investment is to give a sum of money to an institution that does not really need it for survival. That really started me to thinking, and I have been thinking about it ever since. There is a lot of sense in what Mr. Perkins had to say.

Does SMU have the chance to be the kind of institution that all of us aspire to have it be in this young, dynamic part of the country? Do we have a chance to pull it off and to end up with SMU as one of the great universities? Some universities emerge out of very humble beginnings. Some universities have a chance, a great chance, and they pass it up because of either lack of vision or undue fear of the future. Some institutions of higher learning never have a chance, and they can never aspire to be pace-setters among the privately governed institutions. It is obvious also that there are some private schools that will die or be taken over by the state. In light of what Mr. Perkins said, such institutions are not worth the effort of trying to keep them alive as private institutions or even to keep them alive at all. It might be money down the drain.

We here in this room, on this campus, have an opportunity, a better opportunity than we have ever had before, because we, today, are *a better investment.* We are a better investment because SMU's early leadership avoided some major mistakes. For instance, we do not have a medical school. I thank the Lord every night before I go to bed that we do not have a medical school. A private university with a medical school today is in real trouble. This is a big problem at Duke, at Vanderbilt, at Emory, and at Tulane. How to perpetuate a great medical school within the resources of a private institution is an almost insurmountable problem to these institutions. SMU did start out with a medical school and awarded a few M.D. degrees, but I appreciate the wisdom of those early leaders who eliminated that expensive school in the beginnings of SMU. And the elimination of those initial efforts to afford a medical school set a very clear example for Southern Methodist University. Henceforth, we would *not* try to be all things to all people. This makes us a better investment today, believe me!

We are a better investment because we have not made the mistake of trying to be a professional "training school." We educate for selected professions, yes, but on top of a liberal arts education. We have kept our liberal arts. Our original humanities and sciences–oriented commitment has never wavered. We are to this day a symbol of the belief that the educated person must be an inheritor of the best in our civilization as well as educated in the knowledge of the great professions. We do not intend to lose this dimension of the educated person.

We are a better investment because we have not made the mistake of doing away with the highest emphasis on good teaching. One of our big commitments is to the undergraduate and to teaching. We have an important research dimension in this university. No university can be a university without a research dimension. I think, however, that we have learned to keep it in balance.

Those are the decisions made a long time ago that enable us to say today that this university is a better investment. Those decisions provide the opportunity which we now have before us. A careful examination of the continuous investments of our friends in this university will convince all of us, I believe, that we are a better investment now than we were ten years ago. By 1973 we will be a much better investment for big money than we are today.

There is a time for every great, disciplined, demanding step. Timing is perhaps one of the most important single factors in any human undertaking. Today is *that time* for this university. Many things are moving forward today. We are in the midst of a great emphasis on library development. We have the number two library in a very large area, second only to the library at the University of Texas, which is number one in the south.

This university has no church hangups, but it does have a very healthy relationship to our sponsoring church body, the United Methodist Church. Demands are not made either way, and there is pride in the relationship.

SMU is the beneficiary today of the loyalty of some very highly prized members of our faculty. One of the greatest sources of inspiration to me is the knowledge that this university has not only attracted but kept some of the nationally and internationally known faculty members whose commitment is right here. I remember one time, not too long ago, when there were fourteen offers to our faculty in the Perkins School of

Theology and we did not lose a single member, although we have lost a couple of them since. There are examples of this fine loyalty in every school on our campus.

SMU is the beneficiary of designing and planning done a long time ago which placed this university on this spot, designed its buildings, selected its architecture. We enjoy the beauty of this campus every day in the year. Some of you know of the great struggle that some universities are having because of the fact that their location does not give them room to breathe and grow. Some of you know about Boston University. It is hemmed in by a river and a highway. Last year, their president said the highway system had decided to go across the Charles River right through their campus. They are actually talking seriously about buying the land rights over those highways. This is their only chance. Another university has to build elevated sections of its campus *over* the traffic and business districts. Think how blessed we are with our well-situated buildings and our spacious green-ways and playing fields.

We want to keep the beauty and quality of this university and underwrite its future.

We are here today to help each other make some hard decisions about SMU's future.

The figure of $159 million was not plucked out of the air. It represents what I call "the trauma of goal-setting." How much is too much? How much is not enough? This amount of money is hard for some people to understand. We had made a preliminary estimate for a ten-year period of around $220 million. We cut it down because we knew a ten-year projection was not valid. We need a more immediate goal. The goal we have selected after careful studies is $159 million. It is a solid goal, with no fat in it. I am sure we have been guilty of not estimating some things high enough. One of the hardest questions a president of a university is asked is, "How much will it cost?" We are seldom right. I remember the story Mr. Fondren used to tell about how he made a quarter of a million dollars one afternoon. His wife quite naturally wanted to know how. President Selecman (1923-1938) needed a new library building. He talked to Mr. Fondren about his dream of a beautiful building to house SMU's growing library collections. Mr. Fondren asked for an estimate of the cost and President Selecman said it would cost about a half-million dollars. Mr. Fondren agreed to give the money, but when he got home he told his wife about making the quarter of a million because he had been prepared to put up $750,000. Of course, Mr. Fondren spent that full $750,000 before he got through, but you can see that goal-setting can be a real problem for presidents.

We have done our best. The board of governors, key trustees working on committees of the various schools, our administrative officers, all have given you a goal we believe we can live with.

Now I must be very frank with you, our trustees.

I must ask you—all of you, each of you—what will it take to achieve this goal?

It will take *trustee* involvement, not just a vote to adopt this Program of Advancement. If you adopt this program and do not get involved in it, *we are sunk.* This is really what happened in May, 1963, and in the months and years that followed. The board of trustees adopted the Master Plan which carried a financial goal of $37 million. But this never became the trustees' campaign. At the next meeting the trustees came to, they asked, "How are *you* doing on *your* campaign?" It really frightened me to think that all of a sudden this very fine challenge was mine!

I do not want you to adopt this Program of Advancement today until you can honestly feel and say: "This is *my* campaign." A personal commitment from you is the only way we can make it. This Program of Advancement will have to take a priority place in your life. Your time, your attention, your thoughts, and your prayers are essential. You are going to have to bird-dog for us; smell out resources; find out who controls them; interpret this university; help us recruit workers; help solicit, ask people for money; and you, yourself, are going to have to give! If the trustees do not feel a willingness to make a sacrificial personal commitment, we cannot convince anybody else.

Should you vote to adopt this program and commit your efforts to raising this money, we will all be in very fine company, for many other institutions of higher learning are also moving to insure their future. Columbia is in the midst of a $200 million campaign. New York University is having a five-year $222 million campaign beginning in May, 1970. Northwestern is having a five-year $180 million campaign; Yale is having a ten-year program for $443 million. The University of Southern California went after $142 million and has already reached $106 million. The University of Chicago exceeded a three-year goal of $160 million. Duke has almost completed $102 million, which is the first phase of their $187 million campaign.

We now ask your serious consideration of this proposal for a Program of Advancement for Southern Methodist University for $159 million.

(The Program of Advancement was approved and adopted by the Board of Trustees on January 8, 1970. At the conclusion of the five-year period, December 31, 1975, $99,495,835.27 in commitments had come to Southern Methodist University. This program was directed by the Commission for University Advancement, with William P. Clements, Jr. serving as chairman until January, 1973.)

CHAPTER IX

The Future

INTRODUCTION

ADVANCING TECHNOLOGY and liberation continued to exert a strong influence on colleges and universities as the decade of the seventies began. There remain certain pressing questions raised during the sixties but never adequately answered. We hear a more diversified town and gown asking, "How should an undergraduate be educated? What should constitute a proper professional education, when knowledge seems to change every two years and professional obsolescence haunts both professional school and industry?"

Indications are that the future will see a leveling off of growth in numbers of college students. The early maturation of the young with full citizenship at eighteen years of age will influence a university's philosophy regarding housing. The immediate future will also probably continue to reflect a buyer's market in faculty with an accompanying growth in stronger faculty organizations to cope with the dislocations a buyer's market feeds. It is still an open question whether stronger faculty organizations will mean stronger control by faculty over who enters the profession of scholar-teacher, and how well prepared faculty members will be both to serve their disciplines and to give academic leadership to their institutions and to higher education in general.

The escalating costs of colleges and universities are bringing about a sharper focus on what is coming to be known as the "ecology'" of higher education—the relationships among institutions of higher learning. The day of complete freedom to go one's own way regardless of what other institutions of higher learning are offering has passed for all but a very few well-endowed universities. Within states and regions it is now no longer a mark of wisdom or even ordinary brightness for educational leaders (professionals, trustees, regents) to go their own unfettered way. There must be a better understanding of interdependence. Without loss of institutional identity and pride, cooperation must be reconceptualized, as both the tax dollar and the philanthropic dollar find their way through the inflation-ridden years of the 1970s.

President Tate, for whom these problems had few new dimensions, declared, with convictions made resolute through experience, the need for reforms.

The Status of the American University

The Underwood Library of the School of Law at Southern Methodist University was dedicated on April 29 and 30, 1971. A symposium on "The Status of the American University" was included in the two-day program. On April 30, President Tate, who was at that time chairman of the Association of American Colleges, opened the symposium. Members of the responding panel included Bryce Jordan, president-designate, University of Texas at Dallas; Norman Hackerman, president, Rice University; Martha Peterson, president, Barnard College; and A. Kenneth Pye, chancellor, Duke University. President Tate's opening statement defined the issues.

THE CONDITION of the American university is subject to much debate today. Archibald MacLeish, in his inaugural convocation address at Hampshire College last fall, referred to this particular period in higher education as "the troubles." It is perhaps sufficient to say that "the troubles" came to us in the decade of the 1960s and have by no means departed. Great changes have occurred both in our society and in our universities. Many issues confront those of us involved at various levels of university life. Our students are concerned. They know that our society decrees an "education" as the necessary credential for entry into the benefits this society is prepared to bestow. Our educators who teach are concerned. Some of them symbolize in their life-styles the values of the life of learning; some do not. Most of them are either involved in change or afraid of it, yet it is all around them. Our educator-administrators are troubled. They must insure that the institution of the university serves its educational goals. The toll is high, particularly among presidents, as they die or resign. Our trustees and regents carry a heavy responsibility as they hold our institutions in trust. And finally, the general public is showing signs of a confidence crisis in an institution into which society has poured literally billions of dollars.

I do not want to be guilty of "crisis mongering," or of "symptom categorizing." We have enough of that depressing business already. I, therefore, propose to select and briefly analyze what in my opinion are the four most important issues facing universities. I believe these issues to be crucial. They offer alternative choices which can take us in different directions, both as institutions and as a society. Unfortunately, some of our most important choices may have to be made before time and experience give us adequate wisdom. My chief concern is that we so understand these issues that we see fairly clearly the alternatives which we face.

The first issue is that of uniqueness. Each institution of higher learning should have its own particular mission. I believe there ought to be Bible colleges, men's colleges, women's colleges, co-ed institutions, big, little, liberal arts, technical, junior, community, state, and private colleges and universities. This rich pluralism serves well the diversity of our land. Yet there are forces from within and from without the university trying to make educational institutions carbon copies of each other. One of the great threats to the growing junior college movement in this country is the pressure to become a four-year college, granting baccalaureate degrees. I have watched with great admiration the wise development of the Junior College System of Dallas County. They have defined their mission well. They know their diverse constituency and are developing educational programs designed to put those young people on a track with some place to go. It is not likely that this fine educational institution will succumb to the pressures usually placed on community colleges.

I have studied with great interest recent reports on the development of a number of new, genuinely experimental institutions of higher learning wtih clearly defined goals. This spring we had the dean of Hampshire College on our campus. That institution is certainly not lacking in uniqueness. What they are doing is not for every institution, but we will all learn from their experiences.

One of the reasons for the threat of sameness is that so many institutions, including universities, do not know what their mission is. The threat, then, is first of all from within. Some writers refer to this as the "mindlessness" or lack of purpose in educaton. Charles Silberman in his exciting book *Crisis in the Classroom* says, "The solution lies in infusing . . . educational institutions with *thought about purpose.*"[1] It is not enough, for example, for a university to inherit a statement of goals, appearing regularly in its catalog, supporting liberal education. It is not enough to offer liberal arts courses. The university as an academic community must define for itself the way in which that particular community will foster learning which liberates the mind and the spirit. This goes much beyond courses offered. Such a process of self-definition must involve the best resources a university has, in faculty, students, trustees, and administration. These leaders, seeing the world as they see it, will bring uniqueness to that institution. Such a process will enable universities to offer differentiated styles of education suited to particular clienteles.

This sense of uniqueness is also endangered by forces from outside the university. These forces, often unconsciously, pressure universities into being carbon copies of each other. Accrediting agencies, in their zeal for setting and maintaining standards, have all too often been trapped into becoming agencies of conformity. National organizations representing special interests work to develop loyalties to academic disciplines and to the professions, to the neglect of the local institutions. As a result, too many colleges and universities are used as rungs in the ladder of unimpeded professionalism. Even foundations, with their tantalizing offers of support for particular interests, subtly pressure for their concerns. Meeting the conditions required by the government for various types of funding adds to the pressures for conformity.

A university has the right and responsibility to define its own particular mission. If it does not carefully think through its own self-definition, it will be subject to an increasing number of outside pressures. If a university does commit itself to its own particular mission in our changing, complex world, it will be able to deal with pressures and serve society in its own unique way.

The second issue has to do with learning. Fostering learning is a university's number one business. Education generally, instead of creating an environment which makes people want to learn, constricts the learning situation so that many young people are discouraged from learning. Teaching-learning arrangements have been taken for granted, for the most part, throughout the history of higher education. The syndrome of texts, fifty-minute lectures, and exams does not kill *every* creative mind, but its deadening effect takes its toll in intellectual dropouts who manage to meet the demands of degree credentialism but little else. A great deal is known about learning, but it is seldom articulated and made the first principle of the learnng endeavor. Many teachers do a "good thing" for their students out of what Silberman calls "professional instinct" but without any deeply thought-out philosophy of learning. How can our universities serve better their primary purpose of fostering learning? Without attempting to produce a definitive analysis, let me make three observations.

We who call ourselves professional educators must tackle the question of *how learning takes place* and understand better what we should be about. Faculties and deans spend endless hours debating course requirements, teaching loads, grading, and degree requirements. This is necessary. However, they seldom debate the prior question of whether learning takes place at all.

We must be willing to *engage students in real dialogue* about their educational choices. I would be the last to say that students have nothing to teach us about their education. I will be the first to say that a good professor who is himself a learner has much to say to a student. Sometimes he needs only to say a few brief words. I remember that kind of brief conversation on this very campus when I was a sophomore. I was on my way to register for a new term and met one of the professors. He asked me what I was registering for and I told him my choice of a major and of my life's vocation—choice's made on the ground that foreign language was not my thing! He looked at me for a long time and then said three little words: "You gutless wonder!" And he turned on his heel and left me standing there. I had been confronted! It was done by a man for whom learning was the greatest challenge of his life. I changed my major—and my vocation.

Members of an academic community, senior and junior scholars, *must help each other to have the right kind of expectations about both the conditions and the disciplines of learning.* Today students sometimes become so concerned with immediate action that they fail to spend enough time learning to deal on a deep level with the issues of life. I heard recently of a creative professor who met some students on campus picking up cans in the interest of ecology. He was not opposed to picking up cans, but he felt he must ask them what kind of expectations they had about dealing with the larger issue of ecology. They could articulate none. This caused the professor to observe later that if students are deeply concerned about the environment, they must be willing to accept the discipline of acquiring knowledge and concepts that will lead to a serious grappling with the problems involved. You simply cannot cope with the problems of ecology without content and tools. This requires that person have a conditioned expectation, serious dedication, training, and discipline. This kind of understanding of the requirements applies to an engineer or to an artist. A great teacher can inspire his colleagues and his junior scholars to catch his spirit of inquiry. The "heureka" experience of Archimedes is here for all!

The University of Chicago catalog succinctly states the purpose of learning at that great university: ". . . it is to free students to explore, for a lifetime, the possibilities and limits of the human intellect. Though we cannot promise to produce educated men and women, we do endeavor to bring each student . . . to a point beyond which he can educate himself."[2] The alternative is something that might be called simply "social processing." But social processing does not compel the learner to reflect. Reflection is the wisdom of learning. The learner is then equipped to become a creative critic of society. Without such critics no society can stay healthy. Such is our obligation as the *enabler* of learning.

The third issue has to do with change.

A basic assumption in higher education is that the structures of colleges and universities are supposed to serve a philosophy of learning. This, however, is all too often not the case in universities. Universities are caught in an academic lockstep which impedes change and reform from within. Many of our degree requirements are set not because they are necessary for an education, but because they protect the vested interests of particular departments. I am convinced that one of the greatest evils in the structure of universities today is departmentalism. There is a growing suspicion that departments exist not to give creative leadership to the teaching of the historic disciplines and demonstrate their place in contemporary learning, but to serve unimpeded professionalism. Other locksteps in a university include the three-hour courses, grading, empty classrooms in the evenings and in the summer, the dogmatism of committees, and the general depressing unwillingness on the part of all too many faculty members and administrators to examine themselves and to change. This makes universities vulnerable both to those who would like to tear them down and to others who seek reforms.

Challenge to our boxed-in condition is, nevertheless, *here!* We are being told we are in boxes that will no longer hold. Perhaps the most vocal questioning has come from students who are dissatisfied with the learning experience. When serious questions are asked about learning, something serious is going to happen to the structures of universities. Students, however, are by no means the most articulate and incisive critics. One of the most exciting challenges to present structures in universities and in higher education in general was the January 1971 Carnegie Commission Report, *Less Time, More Options: Education beyond the High School.*[3] The Commission's concerns have been reflected in numerous other writings. It is the conviction of those who presented this report that, among other things, undergraduate education can be reduced in length by one-fourth without reducing quality; young people should have wider options for both education and jobs as they move out of high schools; the present college credentialism in our society is too limiting; and education is a lifetime job and need not start immediately after high school. In short, higher education is in need of major reforms. It must be more flexible in structure, more efficiently managed, and more responsive to students and to society's needs.

Those who have been associated with universities for many years generally agree that "self-scrutiny" is something institutions of higher learning simply do not do very well. These institutions can and do study almost everything else, from the natural environment to all manner of other institutions foreign and domestic. They should be able to study themselves, if reform is not to be mindless.[4] The alternative is a fragmented university open to exploitation from without. There are groups and individuals in our society willing to do the scrutinizing for the university, but this represents a surrender on our part that can mean a tragic loss both to the university and to society. Trustees and regents must be aware of crucial *educational* issues. They must appoint first class leaders to positions of power and responsibility. Faculties are going to have to provide energetic self-reform.

As universities move through these challenges, defining their mission, possessing a philosophy of learning upon which to rebuild a structure, they can move into the twenty-first century fully able to serve the society which sustains them.

The fourth issue is the role of the university in the great social problems of our times. Our society is being forced to cope not only with the normal strains of an industrial society, but with all other problems

specific to this time. I am assuming for this audience an adequate awareness of these social problems. I raise the issue of the university's involvement because I hold the basic assumption that the university, as a part
of society, does have a very important role to play in society's dealing
with these problems. It is necessary, however, to find the right balance
between involvement in the affairs of society and detachment from them.
This is no easy dual responsibility. Providing society with the knowledge
and help it needs and demands can be very consuming. This demand
must be balanced with what Robert Nisbet describes as a "nourishing
and protecting" job. There are, as all of us know, fragile, life-giving
activities within the university that are not primarily concerned with
giving advice to society.

It is certainly within the great tradition of universities to be in the
thick of things, continuously related to the powerful currents which
have influenced and altered thought and life. The involvement goals of
a university, however, must be *educational* goals. Basing our efforts upon
the assumption that there is such a thing as the conscience of knowledge,
we must give society young leaders capable of understanding complex
problems. These future leaders of our society must know that such
complexities will not be solved with simplistic slogans. Such future
leaders must be educated to use with competency the tools and methods
by which man comes to grip with difficult, complex problems. Our country needs, in the decades ahead, young people capable of long-range commitment to the solutions of social problems.

There are other major issues I have not mentioned here. The financing of higher education today is such an issue. I believe, however, that
purpose and function well defined and carried out will be the first step
in restoring public confidence and solving our present vexing financial
problems.

With today's college students seeking instant solutions, and with
far too many faculty and administrators rooted in yesterday, we must
find a way of thinking and speaking together about the future. The
American university *is* in danger of having its rich pluralism poured
into a common mold. It *is* in danger of forgetting that learning is its
chief concern. It *is* in danger of losing the right and responsibility for
reform from within. It *does* exist in a society deeply and seriously in
need of the particular gifts of a true university. This, then, is the condition of the American university in contemporary society.

The history of American higher education, however, will not allow

us to close on a negative note. The history of change has been very re-
assuring. We have had much disunity and disorder caused by strong
partisanships which converted us into spoils and prizes. But on the whole,
universities have taken possession of themselves and their destinies—
monitoring, sacrificing, transforming, proceeding often at an uneven pace.
Reform movements within universities have aimed high and low and
wide. Responses have been massive to historic changes in our country,
sensitive to the freedom costs of the old order as well as the incoher-
encies of the new.

Universities have a history worth remembering. As keeper of the
memories of society, the university will not protect itself if it is forget-
ful of its own. Universities are never complete, never finished. They are
forever in the process of being made, and the makers are people, you and
I and all the other people who put their minds, bodies, and worldly
goods to the task.

CHAPTER X

The President's Churchmanship
And His Personal Faith

INTRODUCTION

EVER SINCE HE MOVED to Dallas in 1945, President Tate has been a member of the Highland Park United Methodist Church. He has served on its official board (now the Administrative Board), and is a past chairman of that board. He was elected to the North Texas Annual Conference from his local church from 1950 through 1970.

The North Texas Annual Conference elected him to be a delegate to the United Methodist Church's quadrennial General Conference in 1952, 1956, 1964, 1968, and 1972, and also to a called meeting in 1966. He has served as a member of the United Methodist Church's University Senate, serving as vice president from 1965 to 1970 and president in 1970-71.

President Tate was elected to the executive committee of the World Methodist Council in 1961 and served on that committee through 1975. In 1976 he was a delegate to the World Methodist Council.

At home in the ecumenical world, President Tate served as president of the Texas Council of Churches in 1959 and was a member of the General Board of the National Council of Churches of Christ in America from 1957 through 1969.

A Call to the Texas Council of Churches

The Texas Council of Churches was organized in 1953. President Tate was its president in 1959-60. On March 8, 1960, at the seventh annual meeting, held in Midland, Texas, he spoke of his concerns for this ecumenical body.

WE ARE HERE in this seventh annual meeting of the Texas Council of Churches to consider the organization and program of this council and to project its life into the future. Most important of all, however, we are here to add one more experience in our search for an understanding of and commitment to the unity which is ours as joint heirs with Jesus Christ and members of his body, the church.

We do not need to be reminded that more has been attempted and achieved during the past half-century to draw churches together and to face up to the issues involved in Christian unity, than in the eleven centuries which preceded our contemporary efforts. Because there is deep within the hearts of Christians a discontent over our present unhappy divisions, there is both the mood and the searching for unity which has found expression in a network of world, national, regional, and local patterns of Christian cooperation.

This network is merely the frame for the ecumenical spirit, through which it can work and live, not a substitute for it. The ecumenical movement can lose its momentum not from any lack of devotion on the part of its devoted advocates but because we may become fretful over our deep and stubborn difficulties—or we may become resigned. Either of these will see our ecumenical effort falter and fail. It is essential, therefore, that Christians face up to and deal with two important challenges to any group which would call itself ecumenical, two challenges from which many of our problems emerge.

The first challenge is: *What is to be the level of our relationships?* For some, the relationship depends on interdenominational cooperation in enterprises which individual denominations cannot carry alone. For others, the relationship thrives through action on common concerns over major social problems. Still others come together to try to understand the theological differences which divide them and work to reconcile these differences.

Each of these relationships is a part of the ecumenical movement, some strengthening unity, some feeding division. Because of the kind of world we live in, we must cooperate if we are to have any kind of effective witness. We live in a world where even a united Christian voice is too weak. While I agree that interdenominational cooperation is essential, it has been called the lowest common denominator in relationships between Christians. Surely, for example, we can all cooperate on a ministry to the parolees or to the migrants or on the use of mass media.

In this kind of world, however, there is another level of relationships which we must foster. We must lend our influence to the encouragement of a sustained association between Christians of different denominations over a period of years so that there will come to our churchmen a deeper understanding of the church which will bring greater appreciation of the diversity of life, work, worship within the church and lessen our stultifying defensiveness about that which makes us different. We must strive to become not a group which *just* cooperates on important projects, or one which *just* works together on social problems, or one which *just* seeks doctrinal unity, but a group which strives to become a real Christian community, where commitment to our common Lord is the central loyalty which unites us. Such a Christian community will, of course, always have its divisions; but as long as there is a striving for the strong basis for our unity to be found in our loyalty to our common Lord, this Christian community can tolerate a great deal of diversity and absorb a great deal of controversial stress and strain. In a word, unless we find this basis for unity, the strain will break mere "cooperation."

A second challenge to the ecumenical movement in general, and one closely related to the achievement of a spirit of Christian community, has to do with *the degree to which our people are involved in the decisions* of our various ecumenical councils. The ecumenical movement as expressed in the life and work of our various councils of churches is threatened today by an increasing imbalance between the role of the professional and the role of the lay and clerical members. We all know how this happens, for it has happened in many denominational groups, social agencies, educational organizations, and many other institutions far less complicated. The larger the organization or institution and the broader the program, the greater the temptation to delegate to professional staff the responsibilities which must be assumed by the members of the group. This applies in a special way to a church group. If we are to build a real feeling of Christian community, it is not enough to have staff and a few people determining policy and making decisions. The entire membership of a council of churches, whether it be a local, state, national, or world council, must be brought along, must be much more adequately involved in decisions. Otherwise, *the few will move away from the many.*

Against these challenges to our ecumenical movement, I now want to focus our attention upon the Texas Council of Churches. While we may express it in different ways—and certainly my way is not that of a theologian or even a clerical member, for I am a layman—I feel that one of our major concerns is the voice of the church in Texas. Does the church speak? What does it say? Who listens? Who hears? Does it matter to those who hear? What of those inside who hear many conflicting voices? What of those deeply outside who hear nothing?

It *is* our business to be aware of the total scene in our state, regarding both the church and its life and the world in which the church exists. It *is* our business to ask how the Texas Council of Churches, representing a great host of churches, can be *not a superchurch* but a responsible part of the Church of Jesus Christ. It *is* our business to strive to understand the Gospel in terms of life today and to state, with piercing clarity, some basic principles about that life. Stating principles is not a simple matter which a small committee can do in a few hours and then go home. We must carefully and prayerfully decide what are the significant areas of concern in Texas, and struggle to speak on those issues as a responsible part of the church to the churches in our state. We must be prepared to give that kind of leadership.

Within this context, I call you to be more than a collection of individual Christians with your own individual causes and concerns. I call you also to remember that true ecumenicity has its greatest hope of fulfillment not in you, but closer to the people, closer to the local church. I call you to be a voice, above the limitations of denominationalism, for the deep concerns of our churches and the communities in which they live and work.

What are the great issues, the deep concerns of our people? I would like to suggest two such major concerns to you today.

First must come *a concern for justice for all persons*. There are members of our various communions who favor a change from the status quo in many aspects of what we call "race relations" in our state. There are others who are opposed to any change in the status quo regarding segregation and the whole fabric of intergroup relations which form the way of life in many parts of the state. There are many others who stand at various points in between. How are we going to speak on the issue of justice for all persons so that church members who fear change will hear? How are we going to speak so that those who work for justice are undergirded? I believe that we have to relate, with firmness and clarity, each person's *understanding of redemption to his affirmation or denial of the dignity of all persons.* It is the height of fallacy to believe that we who go to church Sunday after Sunday are in a "saved relationship" to God our Father if we say and do nothing in a society which violates the dignity of persons and shouts defiance at the sovereignty of God.

A second deep concern of our time which we as Christians face is *the challenge of communism to persons of faith.* Perhaps one of the most graphic descriptions of our total world scene today is contained in these words: "poles of power." We do live in a world of growing Soviet military might and our constant attempt to maintain the balance of military power. We do live in a world of growing Soviet economic strength and their claims of the ability of the communist system to give material well-being.

If, however, we have no basis upon which to compare communism and democracy other than that of the materialism of military and economic might, we are indeed in a sad way. We must, of course, maintain a strong balance of military power in the present world situation. Such a balance of power, however, merely buys us time. We will be naïve if we think this military balance alone will win in the long pull. If there is one appalling reality in our life today it is the woeful inability of many of our people, both in the church and out, to come to grips with the key issue which is at the heart of the difference between atheistic communism and Christianity, between communism and a free democracy. That issue has to do with our understanding of history and our conviction about the future. As Christians we deny the economic and materialistic determinism of Marxism. We will not accept the theory that forces beyond our control move with deadening surety upon the pages of history. We believe that as created sons of a Sovereign God we have been given the privilege and responsibility of choice—personal and group choice. We believe that these choices have the power to alter the course of human events, for good or bad. We believe that God acts in history, to help and to judge, through persons and nations, to realize mankind's fulfillment. God acts in our day, even as he did in the days of Moses, Jeremiah, Ezekiel, Jesus of Nazareth, Paul of Tarsus, Augustine, Luther, and Wesley.

However, there can be no direction of the events of history if there is apathy and a surrender of individual, group, and national responsibility. As we daily assume our responsbility to God and to mankind, our way of life has potential moral and spiritual resources equal to the world challenge which awaits us even now. These spiritual resources will give us a healthy respect for the size of our fight, but will free us of demoralizing fears.

With this basic understanding of the differences between atheistic communism and Christianity, how do the Christian church and the Christian citizen fight communism? We fight it by not becoming like it. We fight it by strengthening the great institutions of our free society. We fight it by producing through our homes and our schools a responsible citizenry unwilling to be led around by demogogues. We fight it by insisting on a free flow of knowledge. We fight it by demonstrating to the whole world that we care for human justice enough to sacrifice for it. We fight it by building a climate in our local communities and in our nation where the distrust and coercion of communism cannot thrive. Most of all, we fight it by living a life totally committed to the God of Jesus Christ, with intelligent, dedicated loyalty to the *ethical implications of the Fatherhood of God.*

These, I believe, are two of the great issues which face the Christian church today and give to the church its great opportunity to be truly the conscience of our state and nation. The solutions of these great challenges are not self-evident. We cannot give simple answers by resolutions. We must speak, however, on these issues in such a way that what we say to the churches and the church people of this State will first of all be heard and understood, and then will help them to decide for themselves the steps they will take as responsible Christians.

"Choose Ye This Day"

At the Commencement of Rice University, Houston, Texas, President Tate was invited to give the baccalaureate sermon on May 20, 1972.

TODAY IS A SIGNIFICANT DAY in your life and in the life of this university. A great university, its scholars, its laboratories, its libraries, its exciting climate of research and confrontation have been put at your disposal. You have heard the voices of the past. You know the issues of the present. You have been enamored by winsome ideas. You have agonized over conflicting contentions. Complexity has made knowing difficult.

Through these experiences you have learned some of the dimensions of truth. You have had an opportunity to know what is beautiful and what is ugly; what is valid and what is false; what is permanent and what has decayed; what is worthy and what is worthless. Does this also mean that your life has a center? Unity?

In the Old Testament book of Joshua, chapter 24, verses 14 and 15, we read:

Now therefore fear the Lord, and serve him in sincerity and in faithfulness; put away the gods which your fathers served beyond the River and in Egypt, and serve the Lord. And if you be unwilling to serve the Lord, choose this day whom you will serve . . . but as for me and my house, we will serve the Lord.

If your life is to have unity, you must choose for your life a "master sentiment." Choose ye this day. In the words of Joshua, you must choose whom you will serve. Joshua was speaking to the tribes of Israel. They lived in the midst of polytheism. Many gods were worshiped. Joshua made his choice clear: "Banish the gods whom your fathers worshiped beside the Euphrates and in Egypt, and worship the Lord. But if it does not please you to worship the Lord, choose here and now whom you will worship: the gods whom your forefathers worshiped beside the Euphrates or the gods of the Amorites in whose land you are living. *But as for me and my family, we will worship the Lord.*"

You who sit in this room this day live, even as Joshua lived, in a land of competing ideologies, clamoring for your prior loyalty. *Scientism* seeks your loyalty. Scientism is a belief according to which only the investigative methods of science can fruitfully be used in the pursuit of knowledge and in the validation of life's experiences. *Materialism* calls you, proclaiming a belief according to which the highest values of living lie in material well-being and pleasure. *Secularism* surrounds you. This is a belief in which social standards and conduct are determined exclusively with reference of present life and social well-being. Various forms of *religious faith* in which life's meaning and a system of ethics are defined offer themselves to you. They range from the mysticism of oriental faiths to the wide spectrum of the Judeo-Christian heritage.

I do not know which of these various ideologies has touched your life, if, indeed, any of them have. A life, however, in which you are incapable of making a meaningful and ultimate choice is tragic. One of the most tragic characters in all literature, to me, is the Stranger about whom Albert Camus wrote. Here is a person who found life's choices and decisions beyond him. As he stood in his cell near the end of his life, he looked out the window and said: "I laid my heart open to the benign indifference of the universe".[1] He was indeed a stranger to life.

Even more tragic than those who are incapable of choice made from life's center are those who make their decisions by default or preoccupation with trivial or lesser things. The best and highest never scream or cry or demand to be a part of you. They must be recognized, courted, and with discipline invited into your life.

Without a compelling *master value*, a person becomes helpless, overwhelmed, a drifter. In the deepest meaning of this day, such a person is unworthy of this hour.

I speak to you today about the great choices of life out of my own frame of reference, the Judeo-Christian faith. It is my belief that the Judeo-Christian faith affirms the supreme worth of the human person. This is an anchor to which can be tied endless life choices. Theologically, we can say that God, by whatever name you choose to use, affirms us as human beings and calls us to affirm others. Psychologically, we understand this to mean that we must love, respect, and honor ourselves or we are incapable of loving, respecting, and honoring our fellowman. This is a great affirmation of life, not life in general but your life and my life in particular. Let me try to say what this affirmation means to me.

First, it means that we are meant to possess our possessions, not be possessed by them. One of the tragic characteristics of humankind in our affluent society is our imprisonment by what we possess and want to keep. If we are meant to be worth more than that which we possess, we are therefore meant to be in charge of our lives, to be neither slave nor slave driver. This affirmation of self-worth gives us a foundation upon which to make life's choices.

Second, we are meant to have our life unfold through a calling, a vocation, not to be possessed by our jobs. It is *that* quality of life which gives you unique distinction and reveals who you are. Above all, your life which unfolds through a calling reveals what is at the center of your life, by which you make life's ordinary and ultimate choices.

Third, we are meant to possess our freedom, not be possessed by the blind forces of economics or politics or power plays. It is not easy to believe that we really can possess such freedom in our modern complex world of constant crises and change. True freedom finds its stability in a faith to live by *which forms the ground of our being*. We know in whom we can believe. Consistent with the faith and life choices of

Joshua, Jesus had a divine sense of the priorities of life when he said: "Seek ye first the Kingdom of God and his righteousness . . . and all other things will find their rightful place."[2] Or as the New English translation states it: "Set your mind on God's kingdom and his justice before everything else, and all the rest will come to you as well."

Choose ye this day!

PART TWO

Interviews

CHAPTER XI

Interviews by John Deschner

On Administration

DESCHNER: Willis, talk to me about administration. A president has his hands full of that. What have you learned about administration before and since becoming president?

TATE: When I came to SMU, I worked under Dr. Lee. He was not an administrator. He was an idol of mine and a great scholar. He was a great educational leader, and the trustees trusted his basic leadership. But the details of administration bothered him. He hated to make decisions and, as you know, decisions need to be made daily—some fairly easy and some very complicated. He would get sick rather than face up to some really difficult problems. I really think the Beaty case killed him. His philosophy was that if you don't face up to the issue, more than likely the issue will solve itself. This was contrary to my eagerness to solve problems. When I became associated with him, I couldn't understand why he didn't try to fix everything by Tuesday. But he was right on a great many things. He waited until things cooled down and then he would appoint a committee. Of course, he was following a president (President Selecman) who was an autocrat. The absence of any kind of firmness or authority or clout was highly appreciated on the SMU campus at that time. Dr. Lee was a good influence on me, but I also came to realize that you really have to nip some things in the bud or catch hell down the road.

DESCHNER: Did Dr. Lee expect you to decide some things he wasn't ready to decide?

Dr. John Deschner is a professor of theology at SMU's Perkins School of Theology.

TATE: Yes, he did, and there were some instances when he asked me to do some work for him so that he wouldn't hear any more about it. You could get any agreeable decision from him like shooting fish in a barrel. These decisions were often not written down, and when I first became president I was told many times, "Dr. Lee told me that as long as I was here I could do so and so." Or, "Dr. Lee told me I would always have this office," and so on and on. It was hard fulfilling all of these promises. I made up my mind at that time that I was only elected for one year and that no one would get a definitive decision beyond that one year from me.

Back to your original question. I had to learn to delegate power and responsibility. That was hard. I wanted people capable of doing their specific jobs, who would keep me informed (I hated surprises in the morning paper) and be a member of the team. Sometimes I had this, sometimes I didn't. Clearly, the hardest part of administration is finding and hiring and keeping those who will serve you and the university well.

DESCHNER: Was Dr. Lee good on money matters?

TATE: No, but he had a great capacity to be loved and highly respected in every level of our culture. Men like Mr. Perkins had sublime faith in this man and gladly gave him money for his dreams for this university. We have a long list of people who committed their resources to Dr. Lee's dreams for SMU. If you look at administration from that vantage point, all who follow Dr. Lee have much to live up to.

DESCHNER: Raising money has always been an important responsibility of the top administrator. Has there been any specific strategy in securing big gifts for SMU from Dallas? You are getting them, but it is a rather new development.

TATE: I have come to appreciate the truth that people give money to a going concern. They must believe that they are investing in something that has a future. When I became president, the major capital gifts to this university including all of its major buildings, with the exception of Dallas Hall, were largely the product of contributions made by Methodists outside the city of Dallas or from the university's own resources. This list included the Fondrens, the Perkinses, the Bridwells, the Mc-Farlins. Dallas Hall was a free-will contribution offered by the people of Dallas at the time the university was founded, to get it here. Some friends of Dr. Hyer helped build Hyer Hall. Erik Jonsson and his friends and colleagues broke that pattern by helping us get the Science Information Center and by helping us remodel McFarlin Auditorium, which then helped us get some money from the McFarlin relatives. Then the Fine Arts Center brought some new Dallas money into the picture. From that time on, we have really been able to tap, I think, some of the great fortunes of Dallas. The Meadows and DeGolyer gifts are examples of magnificent donations. We know now of plans for other bequests in which Dallas money will be poured into this university. I think they felt SMU really wasn't worth it to start with. Their eyes were on more prestigious institutions. But now it's a different story and I am grateful.

On the Faculty and Teaching

DESCHNER: I have often heard you say in your addresses in McFarlin Auditorium, at convocations as you open the university every fall, that you have regarded the faculty as being the prime asset of the university. I also know that you have been willing to tolerate some financial liabilities in order to keep and develop that faculty. I suspect that you bought a lot of financial problems for the university at the cost of not slowing up faculty development. I would like to know a little more about that story.

TATE: I think I can sum it up by saying that the challenge of budget-making every year was to find out how much money we could put into the faculty. Aside from annual fixed controls, every year we attacked the budget with one primary concern: how much can we finally come up with for faculty in salary raises and in good appointments? We had reached the place where some of the best graduate schools and their top departments in this country were saying to their graduates, "If you can get into SMU, go." This changed many things—most of all our expectations of the kind of faculty we could have.

DESCHNER: I think there is a sort of popular impression that during your administration we built the campus, physically. We built buildings. I suspect that this wasn't the first priority in any sense, nor was it perhaps historically the major achievement of your era. My guess is that the real building was done on the faculty. Did you have a strategy?

TATE: Yes, a rather simple one, but troublesome. We were able to find some racehorse deans.

DESCHNER: When did you strategize this thing in your own mind?

TATE: I had seen what had happened in the School of Law with a racehorse dean. I had seen what had happened at Perkins School of Theology with another young racehorse dean. I saw him attract you and a bunch of other young potentially great guys around a very gone-to-seed seminary presided over by an old man who liked it the way it was. We had this in not all, but too many of the schools of this university. In one school we had a dean who had the longest active tenure of any dean in the United States, and he did not have a single Ph.D. on his faculty. My strategy was clear and simple: find the deans and hire them. This was not easy to implement because it cost a lot of money. When they came, they were hard to control, but they built peaks of excellence for this university. They built these peaks of excellence by building great faculties in our various schools. We have never been the same since.

DESCHNER: Do you think the character of the faculty has changed in the last twenty years?

TATE: In my generation as undergraduate and graduate student and my early years in administration, I knew faculty members who gave their lives serving, through their academic disciplines, this university. What happened to the institution was important to them. I have watched this change in academia. It seems to me that faculty members are now primarily loyal to their academic disciplines and to the peer judgments of others in their academic disciplines across the country and around the world. A faculty member in engineering may not care about what you, John, a fellow professor at SMU, think about him, but he is anxious about what his colleagues at Stanford or the University of London think about him. This university is just simply something to give him support in his professional advancement. Our retirement plan was originally built not for the traveling professor, but for continuity in faculty leadership here.

DESCHNER: Is this shift in loyalties one of the prices this university paid for moving into the mainstream of university life across the country? Is this not a national phenomenon?

TATE: Yes, I think it is. At Harvard, you can be a Harvard professor and never quite get over into the Yard. At Columbia, during their difficult crisis in 1968, they had no conversation channels between any of their schools. They had not had a general faculty meeting in fifty years. When they needed the hard core of *university faculty*, they just didn't have one. This is true in so many of the larger universities. Faculty members coming out of highly identified graduate departments do feel strong academic discipline loyalty and none or very little to institutions that employ them. One educational friend of mine told me of going after an entire department in another school. He got it. He bought it. But those new faculty members had no loyalty to the university that bought them and would faint if they were asked to serve on a *university* committee.

On the other hand, let me quickly say, I think the thing that has kept me more encouraged through the years was the fact that there were so many new faculty people who were choosing to stay at SMU. Conditions coalesced to encourage longer commitments. Perhaps one of the strongest encouragements to stay longer was that the new faculty found stimulating colleagues here.

DESCHNER: Do you think there has been any significant change in the faculty's skill as teachers? Are we getting better or worse teaching, primarily from the undergraduate point of view, than we were twenty years ago?

TATE: On the whole, I think teaching is better because we have more exciting, better prepared students. But it's a very mixed picture. About the time you hear some really wonderful reports, you hear some things that just curdle your blood. I used to pick sixteen or twenty seniors just before dead week in the spring and have them come to my house for dinner—no deans, nobody else. I would say, "You are all leaving; I'm stuck; give it to me. Who is the best professor you have had?" I have often wished I could have taped some of the answers they gave me. Some of them would open up about what happened to them sitting at the feet of Dr. So-and-so. You could just feel what they had caught in the excitement of learning. But then they would begin to open up on the professors who read the textbook to the class and some other things you wouldn't believe in these modern days. They would get hung up on why tenure allows the university to keep old So-and-so who everybody knows is a fake and a farce, and then lose a fine young good teacher because he didn't publish. That's hard to explain to students. We're not very good at judging what will *keep* a good teacher good as he or she grows older. I've learned that one of the first questions a good prospective dean asks is what percentage of the faculty is tenured. This tells him how much leeway he has in building.

DESCHNER: Is the faculty making any progress in protecting its own quality?

TATE: I'm not sure. I have been worried about the professionalism of education and the academic man or woman. We have attempted, as you well know, to protect their freedom to explore truth wherever it would take them; but there really is no agency to correct the situation caused by those who misuse their freedom, who slough off or go to seed. The administration of a university is really not allowed to. The AAUP (American Association of University Professors) makes fine statements on this, but doesn't seem to have any corrective clout. The ministry has a way of continuous judgment on its members, even to the point of defrocking some in the best interests of the church. The American Bar Association has ways to remove somebody from practicing law. The law profession is fairly well self-policed from within the profession. And if there is one thing doctors don't like it's a quack and they go to great lengths to get rid of the quacks. I continue to ask myself, "Do the professional teachers feel accountable for the quality of their profession?" I have always hoped that our Faculty Senate or even our AAUP chapter would find some way that would seriously police their own professional peers, particularly where they find sloth and incompetence and especially abuse of students, and that they would be as eager to remove such teachers from the professional ranks as they are now to protect those teachers and cover for them. Of course, they will always point to the bylaws of the AAUP and our own university bylaws which state that anybody can be fired after due hearing. But the few cases across the country I know about take years and years and cost half a million dollars' worth of hearings—and you know, we finally get chicken on that ourselves and say that it is really not worth the effort and cost. So we wait them out.

The problem, of course, is that some of a university's finest faculty leaders who know this is true and know the responsibility rests with the faculty itself are not themselves willing to give up the time they want to spend on their own creative teaching and scholarship. That's not hard to understand. So, that's the way it goes.

Fortunately, we here at SMU have few of these kinds of problems. I am talking about a principle rather than personalities.

DESCHNER: Would you mind describing some favorite teacher, maybe someone who didn't teach you but whom you knew about for qualities which you find excellent in a teacher?

TATE: I can think of a name right now, right here at SMU, without any trouble! He has all the qualities. First of all, he really loves his students. He can tell you right now where every one of his pre-med students went to medical school and how well they are doing. He personalizes his relationship to his students. He cares about them. He sees in them great potential even when they are freshmen. He doesn't look down on his students; he looks up to them as potentially great people. Then, perhaps second, he really thinks his discipline of learning is important to learn. He is so personally excited about what he teaches that he makes it contagiously exciting to the people he teaches. He is a hardworking professor. He never lets himself go into a classroom unprepared. And he lives on the growing edge of his academic discipline. He has never stopped learning himself.

I can mention a few others by name because they are not living, physically, any more. Dr. Van Katwijk was one of the great ones. His students (including my wife) became a sect of people who worshiped him because he taught them so perfectly about the beauty of music. There is a Van Katwijk Club, and there is a Junior Van Katwijk Club of people who were taught by people who were taught by Dr. Van Katwijk!

Professor John McGinnis would be another great example of a person who was a great teacher. He had such a beautiful sense of curiosity. Curiosity and a great memory. He could excite a class with the richness of his mind and his spirit. Have you ever read the autobiography of William Lyon Phelps? He taught literature at Yale, and in this book he tells about things that were exciting to him. I remember especially what he said when he first saw the Mississippi River. I suppose I remember it because when *I* first saw that river, I said, "It sure is muddy!" *Not* Phelps. He got out of his car and walked down to the bank and put his hands in the water of that great river and said, "At last, I have seen the place that Mark Twain wrote about." In this one statement, he caught up all the great vision of this great river and the romance and excitement that he had lived through all these years in the experiences of Mark Twain. Phelps was a great teacher because he had so many curiosities. So many things excited him, all the years of his life.

On Academic Freedom

DESCHNER: Willis, a great deal has been written about you and the Gates affair of 1958, but I want to explore what *you* think about it. I came to SMU in 1956, and the first thing I knew about your presidency was when you allowed John Gates, a Communist, to come and speak on the campus. What are the important ingredients of defending academic freedom in the university?

TATE: I have always tried to talk about the university as a place where we deal in ideas. It is the marketplace for ideas. The Gates situation was a great turning point because the mood of the times had a very heavy reactionary John Birch flavor here in our community. We had a lot of frightened people; and the frightened people were the moneyed people. This brought to our community every sort of crackpot national person. They came down here to frighten the people so they would give money to these crackpots to keep their hate campaigns going. That was the climate.

It seemed necessary that Gates be allowed to speak on the campus. We learned some things in all of this. The most important thing we learned was that helping the university to win this battle made it easier down the line. People found out that no organized effort would control us, and we gained strength.

DESCHNER: Did anyone ever accuse you of disloyalty yourself?

TATE: Oh, yes, I was accused of being either a Communist or a sort of dupe. I think the prevailing thought was that I was a dupe rather than a card-carrying Communist—but I certainly was thought of as a dangerous element. I was the only one they knew by name on the campus.

But the whole Gates affair came off fine. We had so much publicity, and the faculty members who crossed ideas with Gates nailed him to the wall. It was a beautiful exercise in how you can talk about things and see both sides very clearly. I was proud of the faculty. When I received the Meiklejohn Award for all this, I realized that some people credited me with more heroism than was true. In actual fact, I took the coward's way out. I couldn't have lived in this university community with all the people who really saw this as an important freedom issue and take any other stand. The real heroes in this affair, I think, were those trustees who had to defend me and the university. Gene McElvaney, sitting down there and taking the hysteria day after day, didn't have wrapped around him the supportive elements which surround this presidential office. He and other trustees really took it on the chin from a lot of frightened people. In the meantime, I was sitting out here on this campus with people patting me on the back. So you see what I mean about who the real heroes were.

On President Tate's Family History and Early Influences

DESCHNER: Willis, I would love to talk to you about your early life and the kind of family history and traditions you came out of. Could you just pick up anywhere and tell me about it?

TATE: When I was a school principal in San Antonio in the early 1940s, my dad, who was a retired YMCA secretary, had just gone to First Methodist Church in Austin to work with Kenneth Pope (later Bishop Pope). My dad became his assistant. Kenneth Pope and Paul Quillian, pastor of the First Methodist Church in Houston, were very close friends. Paul Quillian needed this same kind of help. His church was too big and cumbersome and he didn't have time for all the administration it required. To make a long story short, he heard about my dad's son, me. Quillian called me up, and this led to a very wonderful association which I thoroughly enjoyed. I was there in Houston for two and a half years before coming to SMU. I was given a license to preach, which I never used for preaching, but I did everything else. I had the weddings of all the Ellington Field boys who were getting their wings on Saturday· afternoon and marrying their girls on Saturday night. I did my share of the funerals, too, perhaps twenty-five or thirty during my time there. If I had stayed with this work, I was on my way to getting my ordination as a local preacher. I had become convinced, in studying my early American Methodist history, that this business of being a local preacher was important in the life of the church. I kept my license when I came to Dallas and transferred it to Highland Park Methodist Church.

DESCHNER: I first knew of your family through your father's friendship with my father, who was a minister in San Antonio at that time. I knew of your father's YMCA background. Is the YMCA important in your background?

TATE: John, both of us had wonderful fathers and they saw a lot of each other in San Antonio. My dad was the general secretary of the San Antonio YMCA. He was a religious fanatic in a lot of ways, and his emphasis in YMCA work was the spiritual emphasis. He was not a participant in the physical activities of it; he was half-blind and could never play anything. But he really felt that the YMCA had a great spiritual mission. I can remember as a little boy passing out the hymnbooks at Sunday afternoon meetings in Beaumont. Though my dad's ideas soon went out of style, I grew up right in the YMCA and it had a strong influence on my own personal life. My dad was also secretary of the ministerial alliance and was active in ecumenical affairs. I think he was the ecumenical image in San Antonio at the time of his death.

DESCHNER: How did your father get into the YMCA work? Did he belong to the John R. Mott generation?

TATE: Yes, and he was greatly influenced by it. My dad grew up in Brooklyn. His father was a well-to-do real estate man and a member of the City Commission of the city of Brooklyn before it became a part of New York City. It was called the City of Churches. Charles Goodell was my dad's minister. My dad's mother's family is described in Goodell's book, *Followers of the Gleam.*[1] The dedication of that book is to Willis McDonald, my dad's uncle in that orbit of Methodism in Brooklyn.

Dad got tuberculosis and his father failed in business. He had to drop out of school. The only thing they knew to do with you if you had tuberculosis was to ship you to the Southwest. So they shipped him to Denver, where he had a cousin. They sent him out there to die. One chance in forty was the prognosis. He had no voice, as the disease had affected his throat, so he learned to whistle and became almost a concert whistler. While he was in Denver he caught scarlet fever. He thought the Lord was being pretty rough on him, but as it turned out, the fever went so high that it killed off the tuberculosis germs and led to his recovery!

He became interested in the YMCA and eventually became a full-time YMCA boys' work secretary. He also had charge of student work, and he used to go up to Boulder where the part-time YWCA secretary happened to be my mother-to-be. She was doing graduate work at Boulder. Billy Sunday came to town, and my dad and my mother met at a Billy Sunday gathering. Later my dad was told by well-meaning friends that if they got married all their children would be runts because of his tubercular history. (My dad used to love to tell this because Robert, the shortest one, is six feet, Jimmy is six feet four inches, and you can see me!) At any rate, he married my mother, the YWCA secretary, and began his life work as a YMCA secretary. He worked here in Dallas, in Fort Collins, Colorado, in Beaumont, and then in San Antonio. When he left Beaumont to go to San Antonio, Hastings Harrison succeeded him in Beaumont as general secretary, and that was where Harrison first knew me. Dad retired in San Antonio.

I've told you probably more than you asked for—and I still haven't answered your question about John R. Mott!

DESCHNER: Let me ask the question another way. I've always been very much interested in the student movement in the era of John R. Mott. Did your dad ever talk about Sherwood Eddy and Billy Sunday, and especially John R. Mott? I knew Mott when he was in his high eighties; in fact, he was honorary chairman of the student movement when I was the general secretary. I was in various conferences with him. He was an experience!

TATE: John R. Mott was a great influence in my dad's life, and more indirectly, in mine. In fact, I grew up with John R. Mott as a patron saint. As you know, he was a pioneering leader in the Student Volunteer Movement, a founder of the World Student Christian Federation, head of the International Committee of the YMCA, leader of the International Missionary Council, and received the Nobel Peace Prize in 1946 —to name only a very few of the things he gave his life to. He was a man of simple faith who believed in the disciplined life. He had a great capacity for loving people and there was a winsome, appealing strength to his character. He firmly believed in the missionary outreach of the church, and he was a great model for young people.

He came to SMU shortly before he died and spoke in our chapel. He led a whole generation of students, and influenced many more. Yes, he was an experience.

On the Methodist Church

DESCHNER: I want to ask you about SMU and the Methodist church. If you were a bishop, what would you want the Methodist church to do about SMU?

TATE: I would want the bishop, first of all, to convey to the Methodist churches in his area the fact that they could have pride in SMU without control of it. It is just as simple as that. They cannot have control of this university. They cannot determine its policies. They have to have faith that this higher education function of their Methodist church is consistent with their philosophy and, I hope, the theology of the church. Unless it can work in that spirit, then SMU is a burden to the church, and the church is a burden to us. But I believe we are working together in mutual faith. There have been people, of course, who believe that SMU is too big and cumbersome to be understood and supported by the church. There have been some who believed that the church must separate our Perkins School of Theology from the university in order to keep it tied to the church. The trouble at Drew University and the University of Southern California's abdication frightened some supporters of our seminary, and they wanted to be sure that this kind of thing did not happen to the seminary at SMU.

However, I felt, as an educator, that SMU ought to have a seminary and I was equally strong in my conviction, as a churchman, that the seminary ought to have the university. I said then, and I still believe it, that the day will come when the *university* will have to defend *its* seminary against the church before the day will come when the church has to defend the seminary against the university. I have been proved right about this on several occasions. We did defend the seminary against hysteria in the church, and we may well have to defend it again on other issues. Southern Methodist University holds its responsibility for theological education very safely.

On the Future

DESCHNER: I would like to probe a little about how you look ahead; how you see the higher education scene in America; what is happening to faculty relations, the "tenure" thing, etc. How do you see it?

TATE: This kind of question deserves more time. Let me give you a few "strokes" on how I see the future. We are going to have some hard times ahead, but we are used to them. We are clearly in a no-growth situation in higher education, in both private and public higher education, in the next ten years. We are not going to be flooded with students, and this state is going to realize that it has built too many institutions of higher learning. Normal inflationary costs will create some real financial problems, but maybe no more than we projected twenty years ago.

"Tenure" is going to be up for grabs. There has been lots of study going into this. The AAUP and the Association of American Colleges did a study, and nobody likes that study because it is really threatening. This is a new day for professionalism. Some administrators I have talked to will welcome the union movement. They like the idea of talking to a committee of five once a year: you do this or else, we do this or else, and that would be the extent of the relationship between faculty and administrators.

Then, there is the growth of research centers, "think tanks" where professors can do their research and not be bothered with having too many students around. This development is a real threat to the nature of the university as we have known it, particularly if you care about the character of undergraduate education. To what extent this will affect SMU is, of course, unclear at this time. We are sitting in one of the most creative, exciting parts of the world. What may happen to colleges and universities in other parts of the country doesn't necessarily have to happen to us. To see our future fully realized we are going to have to hustle for good students, hustle for solid support, and keep our vision clear on what we want to be in our particular spot in this country. All of this should make for an interesting future!

CHAPTER XII

Interviews by Gerald McGee

On SMU's Presidents

MC GEE: You've known three out of the four SMU presidents who preceded you in office. What have been some of your impressions of these past presidents with reference to their special contributions to SMU?

TATE: I remember President Hyer from a distance. I was on the campus while he was still teaching. It was one of my great regrets that I did not have a chance ever to have a conversation with him. I knew people who did know him and they talked about him as contemporaries, so I felt that I came to know him, even if indirectly. President Hyer was a great dreamer and planner. He had a quality about him that will always evoke deep respect. He was symbolic of the beauty and majesty of Dallas Hall, a building he built without any money, on faith. He appointed great teacher-scholars like McGinnis, Shuler, and Schuessler, the great academic giants who came here to this Johnson grass field to start a university. I think President Hyer went back to teaching because he really couldn't raise money and he wasn't very good at management. He was a teacher and scientist and planner. But the university's administration got away from him and the debts grew. However, he had already given the hallmark of quality to this university, a great heritage.

President Boaz, later Bishop Boaz, became a really close and honored friend of mine. In fact, my brother married his granddaughter, so I always claimed kin to him. He was one of the great money-raisers of all time. He was one of the very few people I ever saw who thoroughly enjoyed asking people for money. I asked him one time why he loved to

Gerald McGee is associate director of Public Relations and director of University Publications at SMU.

go see people to get money for SMU, and he said, "Well, I know I'm going to heaven and some of my best friends I'd like to get to heaven too, and their best chance is by supporting SMU." He was an enthusiastic, contagious developer of our dreams for SMU, and I think his best service to the church and to the university came after his retirement. He retired, I think at the age of seventy-two, as a bishop, and worked on long after he was ninety in the development of SMU.

Then President Selecman, later Bishop Selecman, came in 1923. SMU was ready for expansion and building and he did it. He organized the Law School and the Engineering School, built the first part of Perkins Administration Building, McFarlin Auditorium, our first dormitories, Hyer Hall. And he secured the money for Fondren Library. He was a great builder.

MC GEE: I have heard from people who knew him that he was the president who turned off all the faucets.

TATE: Yes, something like that. But you must remember that he had a difficult time as president during the depression years. In spite of those lean years, he really accomplished a great deal.

When President Lee was elected in 1938, he understood in a special way the need for quality in the academic program. He had a great capacity to interpret this, and the money came in because the people believed in him. Even though he didn't like administration, he really made a great university out of this place because he knew what to emphasize. He knew the importance of strengthening the library system. He believed in standards. The chapter of Phi Beta Kappa came to SMU during his tenure as president because of the quality of our educational program. He was in the right place at the right time.

I think SMU has been blessed in the presidents who came at the right time in its history to give the right emphasis. At least, I can say that about those who preceded me. It's important for the university community under the leadership of the trustees to determine what kind of leadership the university needs at any given time when leadership is changing. At the end of my presidency, I was very sure about not having anything to say about who would follow me. I think every president ought to represent some contrast, based on the institution's needs. There were things I had neglected, and there were things I did not emphasize that a new president ought to come in and give leadership to, just as I took up some things that Dr. Lee had neglected. And he took up some things that Selecman had neglected, etc. It's too bad if you have a succession of carbon copies in the presidency. I have learned to appreciate the contributions each past president has made and I am very well aware of the fact that each of them had problems, and each of them had deficiencies. And that makes me realize that I was supposed to have my share of them, too!

On Working with Trustee Leadership

MC GEE: Dr. Tate, you have had some very forceful leadership in the chairmanship of the board of trustees and its executive committee, now called the board of governors. What kinds of relationships did you have, especially with the executive committee leadership? Were they hard partners?

TATE: Let me start with Gene McElvaney. He really was a very understanding man. When I became president, Gene was an experienced trustee. He had great knowledge and grew to have much more. In addition, he had great love for SMU. This made him a great partner. Of course, he had a short fuse on some things. One of his great obsessions was the oil depletion allowance. He didn't want that stepped on by anybody. Not very often, but a few times, I had some defusing to do. Of course, he knew the role of the trustee and he never touched administration. He always expected me to be the administrator even when he couldn't understand some of my reasons. In things he couldn't understand or couldn't accept, he would have enough faith to know that I knew what I was talking about. Gene sat down at an exposed desk in the heart of the city, and when we would have one of our regular controversial crises he had to take the beating, day after day, of people who wouldn't have the guts to come out here and see me. Sue still takes it from some people who don't know any better, but she stands up to them just like Gene did.

Gene had the admiration of the board. He really was a leader of the board. They learned to depend on him. I think the board gave to Gene more power on investments and Gene gave me more authority to decide things and get them done than either of us deserved. We should really have had more checks and balances, but it turned out well. He was chairman of the committee that nominated me to be president. I told

Bishop A. Frank Smith, then chairman of the board of trustees, that I would agree to accept the presidency if he would stay on as chairman and Gene as chairman of the executive committee. They agreed and this gave me the assurance, the backing, and the guts that I would have to have. He defended me through thick and thin times. It was a great relationship, and we became very close friends. We were never close social buddies. I never did buddy in his private social life, and he didn't in mine; but when it came to SMU, he gave me priority in his time and energies. I think he was close to being a prime example of what a trustee of an institution of higher learning ought to be.

I was fortunate in developing much the same kind of relationship with Bill Clements, who followed Gene as chairman of the board of governors. Bill was a late comer to trusteeship in higher education, but he made equally good progress in understanding the requirements of trusteeship. Gene had a little more flexibility in judgments. Bill tended to be more black and white, but you could get through to him. I used to kid Bill, you know—he would say, "I'm unalterably opposed." And I would say, "Well, this means that it will take me two weeks to convince you," and he would laugh. He knew I'd take the two weeks! He had faith that I knew what I was doing, but he also believed that I didn't know what I was doing in some fields, and he was right about it. Investment policies, for example, was an area in which I had no competence, and I had nothing to say. A good trustee committee handled that. But by the very same standard, Bill was willing to acknowledge my special competence in university administration. He wasn't quite as good as Gene in staying out of administrative decisions. He wanted to get in and really know, and he would make me defend my decisions harder. On inviting Martin Luther King, Jr. to speak on the campus (or rather in supporting the campus committee which invited him), I almost lost Bill. "You can't do this to Dallas and to SMU," he said. But then he took the time to come out to McFarlin Auditorium and hear King speak to an overflow crowd. He came to me afterward and said he was mistaken. He said, "That's the greatest sermon on love I ever heard." He told this all over town.

Bill was eager to learn. He wanted to be a good trustee of a university—and he loved SMU. He has told me many times that he could take teaching from me because I took him as he was. I have to admit that I'm humbled by this. He never ceased to thank me for his growth as a university trustee, and a great affection developed between us. Just like my relationship with Gene, we moved in different social circles. But in the orbit of Southern Methodist University, we shared a great life.

He gave SMU first call on his time and energies, and he was a great chairman of the board of governors.

On the Ups and Downs

MC GEE: What are the things that have stuck with you all the way, in your ups and downs?

TATE: Let me mention a few. First there were the satisfactions I felt that SMU continued to be a free university, an open university, which was an obsession of mine; that this was a place that was a happy place to work. We had our share of jealousies, of course, and a lot of incompatibilities, and I even had four or five people I really couldn't work with. They were good people, fine in their fields, good in their assignments, but they just brought out the worst in me, and I am sure I did that with them. But, on the whole, I have had almost the richest satisfaction in the reservoir of very great personal loyalty given to me and to this institution. Nothing gave me a more constant buoyancy than the assurance of this. Mrs. Perkins used to write me a letter that would arrive just when things were darkest, and she would say in her own special way, "hang in there." I'd get a Christmas card from an undergraduate saying "You're OK" in his own words. This cost him only eight cents and a little time. There was an awful lot of this, and I responded to it. If I had been in a situation—and I know they exist—where you just hated to walk into a building because you knew you were right in the middle of a backbiting or knifing situation, I couldn't take that. There is a long list of people I have really loved and depended on. Their often unexpressed love and faith that we were on the right track and that I could count on them all the way meant more to me than I can say. If I hadn't had that kind of steady support, I believe I would have broken.

I remember especially a letter I received from one of our really great faculty members, on his retirement, thanking me for so much. He recalled our early struggles to make SMU a fully integrated university, when some were pushing us toward the millennium and others were urging us to retreat back to Jim Crow. Let me read you this paragraph.

It feeds me every time I read it: "I remember my impression then of your steadiness and confidence—and your equal concern for both the right course and the prudent one. And this impression has remained ever since: your equal commitment to academic freedom and progress with a sensitivity to unobtrusive and unabrasive ways of getting things done, in the implementation of the same vision that we've all shared together but which you had the administrative responsibility for implementing."[1]

MC GEE: When I think of integration at SMU, I always think of your overpublicized meeting with the black students in May, 1969. When did integration begin at SMU?

TATE: Integration at SMU took its first steps in 1950 under the leadership of Dr. Lee. The action of the board of trustees on November 10, 1950, started the process of integration. There are no public statements about integration. The university followed a strategy of quiet but positive progress toward making SMU a university open to all who could meet its admission standards. I believed that we would get more done if we did not debate it or confront people with it. I explained to the trustees that I was assuming they expected me to deal with desegregation and integration and that unless I was instructed otherwise, I would deal with it at the pace I believed best. We lived through a good many "firsts"— the first athlete, etc. And so we moved quietly. I had some exceptionally fine help from faculty, staff, and students. I remember so well how the students protected our first black young woman student from exploitation by the media. And I will never forget the steady defusing here and there we had to do when Jerry Levias was here trying to get a good education and play football. Sometimes it got rough. Jerry was told once that he would be shot if he appeared on a certain field in another city, but he went ahead and played.

We've had some exceptionally fine minority students, and one of the reasons for this is that SMU was one of the earliest universities in the country to begin and to continue the Upward Bound Program.

MC GEE: With this slow steady progress toward openness, why do you think you were confronted by SMU's black students in 1969 with a list of their special needs?

TATE: By 1969 we had a good group of black students on campus. I think I must confess that we were somewhat naïve. We had thought that all we had to do was to take away the barriers that were keeping black students out of SMU. We thought that opening the doors would automatically bring the solution. It did not, fully. We found that really very fine black students were angry because their life on this campus was not fulfilling. I was disappointed to learn this. But we had such fine, dedicated, reasonable young black student leaders, and they helped me to understand that while they were pursuing their education, they also felt a deep need to explore and cherish their own ethnic heritage and express that heritage in their lives. In the same exchange, we helped them toward a better understanding of what a university could be expected to do and what it could not do.

We had no complete victories. We just did the best we could.

On SMU and Conflict with the Community

MC GEE: Sometimes SMU's commitments as an educational institution have at least given the appearance of being in conflict with the larger community in which it is located. Are these conflicts significant? If so, what would you consider the best way to resolve them?

TATE: I think it is the nature of a university to be in conflict, at times, with its community and society at large. A university has to be conducive to invention and change and new ideas. While everyone is very happy about the notion of *progress*, on the other hand, the notion of *change* really is a very uncomfortable thing for many people to face. When we have an institution whose business is to examine critically our society and the value system upon which we as a society base our decisions, you must expect change or the possibility of change. This can be uncomfortable. But that is what a university is. That's what it does. If the university were nothing but the reflection of its outer community, it would not serve that community and would, itself, eventually die.

To answer your last question, there is no way to resolve these conflicts, if by resolve you mean do away with them. But there are many ways to help the community to understand the nature of the university and the ultimate benefits which come to the community from the university's inventive services to society.

MC GEE: Has SMU's environment changed in the last twenty years? Are the geographic region, the economic mix and the temperament of the people, the stresses, the demographics, more or less conducive to the further growth of a first-class academic institution here?

TATE: Yes, I do believe the environment is different from the environment of twenty years ago. There is more understanding and acceptance of pluralism in our city and our area than there was when I first became president of SMU. I think this community did a turnaround after the assassination. The press did, and they helped the community. We don't like to talk about the assassination even today, but it helped this community to become more open. Everything isn't black and white. There are a lot of factors that go into building a good community, and a person or a group simply cannot make scapegoating a way of life. We have learned to live with pluralism—creatively, I hope. This has been the strength of our country and the strength of our heritage. We can find a way to live without everybody having to be alike and to agree on everything. The university was a pioneer in this, and it tried hard to be a leader in this concept of pluralism.

To answer your question specifically, yes, the climate of this community and its surrounding area is clearly more conducive to the further growth of first-class academic institutions, not only SMU but others as well.

On Major Accomplishments

MC GEE: If I were to ask you to list the three top accomplishments during your years as president of SMU, could you make that judgment?

TATE: I would find it difficult to name accomplishments. That must be a judgment of history. I take pride, however, in many things. Clearly the major developments, in my estimation, were: first, the growth of SMU's faculty, both in number and in quality; second, the improvement of SMU's student body with the inauguration of Selective Admissions, which was begun as an idea under Dr. Lee in 1952, was approved by the board of trustees in November, 1955, and became operative in September, 1956; and third, the continued support, on the part of the board of trustees, of our faculty on the issue of academic freedom.

CHAPTER XIII

Interviews by
R. Richard Rubottom, Jr

On Selecting Presidents

RUBOTTOM: Willis, I know you have observed—and served on—a variety of search committees working to fill important positions in higher education including the position of president. Were you groomed for the presidency of SMU under President Lee? How did you come to be president?

TATE: First, let me describe how I happened to be at SMU. I had known Dr. Lee for a good many years while I was getting both my undergraduate and my graduate degrees. Dr. Lee was soon to be in need of a dean of students. He was quite specific when he asked me to come as assistant dean, with the view of becoming dean later. He wanted someone who knew SMU. He was looking for an SMU graduate. So I came as an SMU-identified person. This was at the time when World War II was ending and the veterans were beginning to come back to school. We were under a great strain as a university. There were trimesters and round-the-clock classes. We had all kinds of housing problems, and I was responsible for solving them.

Later it became apparent to Dr. Lee that SMU needed a development office. Bishop Boaz was raising a little money by asking people to support the Sustentation Fund which he had started. But there was really no organized attempt at public relations or any kind of development. I think Dr. Lee felt that somebody who was kind of red and blue and had been identified with SMU for a good many years could help in the interpreta-

---

Dr. R. Richard Rubottom, Jr. is professor emeritus of political science, former director of the Center of Ibero-American Civilization, and former vice president of SMU.

tion of the university's needs and could organize money-raising. He asked me to give up being dean of students and become vice president and try to organize a system of development. I moved into that work in 1950. Then Dr. Lee became ill and the three vice presidents had to make many of the decisions. This was the way I came into central administration. After Dr. Lee's resignation because of his health, the trustees appointed a committee to recommend a new president—and you know the rest of the story.

RUBOTTOM: Twenty years have passed. How does one prepare to become a college or university president today? In terms of the background that is being sought today for top-level administrative posts, would the background you brought to this position square with what a search committee asks for today? Do you feel that formal preparation for high-level administration in education can be found at the educational level, or do you feel such preparation can be hammered out in some other way? Or is there a combination of both? How do you prepare to be a college or university president?

TATE: I suspect I will have to give you an indirect answer. When it became apparent that Dr. Lee could not continue to function because of illness, the trustees, who had great admiration and love for Dr. Lee and the momentum he had brought to this university, were very sensitive to the fact that they did not want to change directions. They did not want a person from the outside. They did not want somebody who would take a couple of years to turn the university around into something different from what it was. Others may give you a different answer, but I think the main reason why lightning hit me was that I happened to be there, was completely committed to Dr. Lee, and was identified with his program and his philosophy of education for SMU. The board of trustees saw this as a way of avoiding a break-in period and the real danger of somebody changing directions.

Whether or not that was a good enough excuse to elect a man who did not have the long preparation and experience they now look for in a college or university president, I do not know. I think what I am saying is that every vacancy in a presidency has to fulfill a specific need for that institution. Sometimes you need an absolute change in direction, and you look for the person whose experience tells you he can meet that need. I think when President Selecman left, Dr. Lee came in with a brand new and absolutely opposite management style and philosophy of education which this university badly needed. I say that without any discredit to

Dr. Selecman. At the particular time that I was elected, the trustees felt this university did not need change. It needed continuity.

Now back to your question about training for the job. A presidency is not an easy position to be trained for. Experience in knowing the life of the college or university is essential. I value highly my teaching experience, my work with students, and my work in interpreting SMU and seeking financial support for it. The American Council on Education's internship program for future college and university presidents is a fine program. A president has to be a good manager, but he must understand the academic life, preferably from firsthand experience. He must understand and defend the academic man and his quest for truth. There are a lot of management people I know in this country who have no understanding at all of the life and work of academic people. When a person does not understand that, he will not make a good president even if he happens to be a superior manager. The other place where I think it is important for a president to be knowledgeable and sympathetic is in understanding the trials and the opportunities of the college years and their influence on the lives of young people. This is virtually impossible to know outside of actual experience on the college or university campus.

On Planning the Master Plan

RUBOTTOM: I remember participating in the development of SMU's Master Plan as a member of the Committee of Fifty while I was still with the State Department. How did all of this major planning effort come about?

TATE: Two or three factors made it necessary. We had been through the veterans' super-enrollment period. We were under terrific pressure from every conceivable place to add more schools and to be the solution for some vocational educational problems. The pharmacists wanted a school; the social workers wanted a school; the nurses wanted a school; and of course, steady pressure from the technological industries around Dallas for more technology. Everybody thought this university could solve their particular problems. It became apparent to us that if we tried to do all of these things, we would buckle under and break our back. We had SMU's fiftieth anniversary coming up. One or two of my staff members laid it on me kind of heavy. Soon I would have been president for ten years. Were we drifting? It became evident that it was the right time for us to plot our course, to stake out our limitations, and to decide our peaks.

We got the serious consideration of a lot of people on the affairs, the problems, and the alternatives of this university. The Committee of Fifty, of which you were a member, was composed of some very distinguished people. We had their undivided attention on what the alternatives for SMU could be. We got everybody on the campus involved, with all kinds of task forces and committees. We picked a faculty committee that dedicated a whole year to dialogue among themselves and with me on what a university really is and what our particular role must be. We had a stimulating man, Jesse Hobson, who was vice president and who was a good dreamer. We had to put some people around him to pick up after him, but he was a great stimulator of thoughts. We started the process of "master planning" by asking questions. Nobody could take a position at first. The best report we received was from a dedicated group of students who tried to project what kind of university they would like to have. We didn't want to take any other university in this country as our model. The process during about eighteen months was thrilling. It was, in a real sense, a new beginning for me.

RUBOTTOM: The total experience of the Master Plan happened from 1961 to 1963, and it was a major university undertaking. What have been the results of this planning, and where do we go from there—now, in the 1970s?

TATE: The more I have looked back on the Master Plan, the more I realize that it was a turning point in the university. We achieved a certain momentum and sense of direction. The most important decisions we made were what we would do and what we would not do. Then we tried to define what we needed in the way of support. We quit trying to be all things to all people, and when we did that I think we were able to show some peaks of excellence. The problem with the peaks of excellence that grew out of the Master Plan was that they left some very deep valleys. Some of these continue to be an enigma today. Also, I am very well aware that what seemed to be an innovation ten years ago could now be old hat, and certainly needs to be reexamined. We need to reexamine the size of SMU, its immediate and long-term goals, its limitations and its commitments, how it all looks now. I don't believe those directions set ten years ago ought to be followed without thorough reexamination now, because conditions have changed. In other words, I am not sensitive about change and I will not feel personally defeated if, for example, the University College goes out of business and they find something better. In the early days, I defended the University College purpose, its original concept, and its structure. Later, as its programs changed, I still supported its purpose. I continue to believe in the educational goals it serves. But any structure can outlive its day.

Beyond the Master Plan, there was always the challenge of continuous planning. I must admit, as I look back, that as important as planning is, I was never able to establish firmly a university office of planning with the responsibility to keep rolling projections in view so that we could always see five years ahead.

On a Philosophy of Work

RUBOTTOM: Willis, how do you handle your job when you can't get it all done?

TATE: You just cannot borrow from tomorrow if you are doing the best you can today. I learned that early in my work at this university. During my term as dean of students, we had no place to put people and we called everybody who had a gas meter in University Park, seeking places to house students. Our problems were so overwhelming we never did quite get them solved. Going to bed knowing that I hadn't finished the job, that it wouldn't get done if I didn't do it, and I hadn't done it, I think I became sort of philosophical knowing that if you do the best you can, the future is going to have to take care of itself. So I trained myself not to borrow time from tomorrow. This enabled me to accept my home as a haven and a good night's sleep as a life-preserving gift. That philosophy has helped me many times during my years as president.

CHAPTER XIV

Interview by Joe Sherman

On Favorite Audiences

SHERMAN: You've spoken to many groups and been extensively interviewed. Who is your favorite audience? Your worst?

TATE: I have always had my greatest satisfaction making a speech to college students when they were with me. New students during freshmen orientation, with their great expectations and their undivided attention, gave me great satisfaction. I suspect that my ability to talk to them diminished through the years because I had trouble understanding their terminology and some of their values—and, of course, the longer they stayed around here, the more they kept me on my mettle.

My most dreaded assignment, I'm sure, was speaking to the general faculty. I long ago stopped trying to explain this.

SHERMAN: What about the media?

TATE: I think I have always felt uncomfortable with the media people. I really had to know what reporter or writer I was talking to. There have been some very good ones. Some reporters loved to get me in a trap—fighting somebody—and they'd have enough copy for a week! But I learned to bleed a little rather than answer back and start a fight.

Joe Sherman is executive director of Information Services at SMU.

CHAPTER XV

～

Interview by
Jo Ann Harris Means

On Students

MEANS: President Tate, SMU has such a variety of students: undergraduates, graduates, professional students. What image comes to your mind when you think of an "SMU student"? Also, what has been your reaction to the changes we have made during recent years in student life on campus, particularly in the rules and regulations for undergraduate women?

TATE: When I think of "the SMU student," I really think of the undergraduate. To answer your second question, I must confess that certain changes in student life have been hard and slow for me to accept because I am of another generation. I grew up in a generation which had an obsession about sexual matters. If there was a bed in a room and two people of different sexes in that room, this was an intolerable situation, because, of course, the bed had only one use. It never occurred to my generation that the best use of a bed was to put the record player on it! I had all that background and it was pretty rigid. I have had to admit that breaking down that rigidity about the life of the undergraduate has been a wholesome thing. It has created a wholesome atmosphere because the old dating that I knew as an undergraduate or as an early dean of students was too rigid. A girl would lock herself up in her room on Saturday night with the light out because she would be afraid that somebody would find out she didn't have a date! Not having a date was the greatest stigma a girl could have. She would not walk across the campus to go to a basketball game if she didn't have a date. Those unwritten rules were so strict. On the other hand, I came into some early experiences as

---

Jo Ann Harris Means, Attorney-at-Law, is a former SMU student leader.

a dean with a good many very, very immature students, particularly girls, who had been kept little girls by their parents. All of a sudden they were thrown into a situation where they had to make their own decisions, make up their own minds, even pick up their own clothes for the first time. I saw this terrible adjustment. I was trying to be protective because when we had great tragedy in some of these adjustments, I always found myself feeling a little sense of guilt that maybe we were to blame.

Now, I realize that paternalism or *in loco parentis* is going out fast. But differentiating between paternalism and genuine concern for an individual student was hard for me. Probably the reason it was hard for me was that I had such a wonderful dad. My dad let me grow up, but there wasn't anything I couldn't share with him. There wasn't any problem I had that my dad wasn't there, available. By the time I got to college, I thought this was a universal relationship between parents and their sons and daughters. So, for somebody to type the university as "paternalistic"—well, knowing my relationship with my father, this was exactly what I wanted a college to be: loving, kind, allowing me to make my own decisions, but nevertheless, available and concerned about my life. I suppose I really thought that everybody's dad was that kind of a person. I found out that this was not necessarily so.

I think I should probably add here that this business of a college being *in loco parentis* could really backfire. We have had some students who have had such a violent reaction to their parents, mostly against fathers, that when they came to SMU I became the symbol of that father. I have really had to take the brunt of some students' real problems with their parents! But these were the exceptions.

I think that on the whole high school students are a great deal more sophisticated now. They are more ready academically and emotionally. They are more mature than they used to be. For example, marijuana was at one time a college problem. It is now more of a high school problem. If students have not come out of high school with some pretty good value choices already firmed up, they aren't likely to make them on today's college campus.

MEANS: Were the students during the "student revolt years" (1966-70) exceptions? Out of the mainstream of students? An aberration?

TATE: I believe that the students of the middle and late sixties were more in the mainstream of the world and its problems than any generation I have ever known. It's true that the excited, noisy students were in the minority. On the whole, the students through that period and even into today are really the most idealistic, the most concerned, and the most knowledgeable students we have ever had here.

MEANS: What about student leaders who deliberately fight the university administration? Do you like to see student leaders show their independence? Do you really have to work at keeping your cool with those who fight you?

TATE: I always advised student leaders, particularly presidents of the student body, that they could not be effective in their leadership role if they came to be known as a stooge of the president. I told them I would respect them in taking issue on behalf of the students, and if they did not take issue with me on behalf of the students, they would not be worth anything to this university community. I tried to explain our relationship by telling our student body leaders about how we play football. You've got some opponents. It's not a personal thing. One of the hardest judgments for an official to make is "interference with the receiver." When the pass is thrown, you cannot interfere with a man who is eligible to catch the pass. The offensive man and the defensive man are both eligible to catch the pass, and any bona fide effort they make to get to the ball is legal. But if you take your eyes off the ball and play the man to keep him from catching the ball, it's interference. Now, you can collide getting to the ball, and it may look like a terrible interference, but if both players are making a bona fide effort for the ball, it's legal. I tried to help a student understand that if his or her efforts are bona fide efforts toward the issues, it's OK. But if a student ever begins to attack the opponent, then he's in trouble. That kind of trouble I've had very little of. We've had a wonderful group of student body presidents. I let them know that I never felt they were being fair with me if they just tried to "yes" me—and they didn't.

Of course, you don't try to talk with the editors of the student newspaper. They can't help thinking you're interfering with their freedom. But their occasional unwillingness even to seek out the facts was sometimes worrisome.

MEANS: Mr. President, we've had some experiences with the press and the media which were a disservice to our students. I'm sure you remember the time we had the Student Center fire and one of our state newspapers reported that SMU students cheered while the Student Center was burning down. You got lots of letters about that. What really happened?

TATE: You must remember that this occurred during the days when there was a great deal of violence across the country and students on a number of campuses were involved. But we just never had anything like that at SMU. The Student Center belonged to the students. They felt it was theirs. I recall very clearly their anguish over seeing something as beloved as that building going up in flames. When that fireman risked his life by finally getting on top of the roof to get water to the flame, the students gave him a very big cheer. They were cheering his bravery and his willingness to risk his life to save their building. Of course they weren't cheering because the building was burning! It still shocks me to recall that story in the paper. I remember the student who came out of the building after he had been inside fighting the fire. When I tried to thank him, he said, "You don't have to thank me. This is my university, too." I almost wept. When the letters came in after that misleading news story, it was a pleasure to answer them.

Appendix

University Growth

	1954	1972
Library holdings	363,571	1,205,878
Special Collections in		
SMU Libraries	15	60*
Full-time Faculty	204	456
Trustees	48 (from 8 states)	77 (from 14 states)
Students		
Undergraduate	3,665	5,501
Graduate	797	2,226
Law and Theology	782	939
Dallas College (downtown)	3,031	1,350
TOTAL	8,275	10,016
Degrees Granted		
Bachelors	703	1,353
Graduate: Masters	136	697
Ph.D.	—	66
Law and Theology	204	224
TOTAL	1,043	2,340

(*) Includes three collections on loan which later became permanent university collections.

	1954	*1972*
Annual Budget	$4,539,000	$30,324,000
Tuition (long-term)	$500	$1,800
Student Aid	$480,000	$5,782,252
Endowment	$6,732,036	$40,289,000
Total Assets	$31,135,073	$137,781,370
Permanent Buildings	48	80

(Sources: *Reports* to and *Minutes* of The Board of Trustees; Colophon's *Special Collections in the Libraries at SMU*; the Registrar's *Blue Book on Degrees Granted at SMU*.)

COLLEGES AND UNIVERSITIES IN THE DALLAS AREA

1954

Southern Methodist University

Arlington Junior College

University of Texas Southwestern Medical School (later, the University of Texas Health Science Center at Dallas)

Established since 1954

1956   University of Dallas

1959   Arlington Junior College became a senior college

1961   Bishop College moved to Dallas from Marshall, Texas

1965   Dallas Baptist College moved to Dallas from Decatur, Texas

1965   Dallas County Community College District organized
        1966 El Centro College
        1970 Eastfield College
        1970 Mountain View College
        1972 Richland College

1967   Arlington College became the University of Texas at Arlington

1969   University of Texas at Dallas

Notes

CHAPTER ONE

1. John Keats, *Selected Poems and Letters* (Boston: Houghton Mifflin Co., Riverside Editions, 1959), p. 261.
2. T. H. Huxley, letter to Charles Kingsley (September 23, 1860), quoted in H. L. Mencken, ed., *A New Dictionary of Quotations* (New York: Alfred A. Knopf, 1946), p. 376.
3. Vitruvius, *De Architectura,* ix, 215, in Stevenson, *The Home Book of Proverbs, Maxims and Familiar Phrases* (New York: Macmillan Co., 1948), p. 802.
4. John Milton, *Samson Agonistes,* lines 20-22.
5. Luke 12:48 (Revised Standard Version).

CHAPTER TWO

1. Section 21 of Vernon's Texas Civil Statutes, Articles 2919e-2.
2. Ibid.
3. Psalm 1:3 (Revised Standard Version).

CHAPTER FOUR

1. Minutes of meeting of the Faculty Senate, October 26, 1955.
2. Minutes of meeting of the Faculty of the College of Arts and Sciences, September 29, 1955.
3. *SMU Campus,* September 30, 1955.
4. Carter Murphy to William P. Fidler, January 28, 1965.
5. Willis M. Tate, *AAUP Journal* (Summer 1965), p. 311.

CHAPTER FIVE

1. *The Master Plan of Southern Methodist University, 1963-1969.*
2. Ibid.
3. John Foxe, *The Acts and Monuments of John Foxe,* 8 vols. (New York: AMS Press, 1965), 3:718-20.

CHAPTER SEVEN

1. Willis M. Tate, "A Woman's Choice," *Key Magazine* (Kappa Kappa Gamma Fraternity) 77 (Spring 1960): 8 ff.
2. Paraphrased from Matt. 7:24-27.
3. Lewis Mumford, *The Culture of Cities* (New York: Harcourt, Brace & Co., 1938), p. 78.
4. Kahlil Gibran, *The Prophet* (New York: Alfred A. Knopf, 1942), p. 18.

CHAPTER NINE

1. Charles E. Silberman, *Crisis in the Classroom* (New York: Random House, 1971), p. 379.

2. University of Chicago catalog, *The College*, 1969-1971, p. 19.

3. Published by the Carnegie Foundation for the Advancement of Teaching, 437 Madison Avenue, New York, N.Y. 10022.

4. For a more complete discussion of institutional self-study, see *The Assembly on University Goals and Governance* (Cambridge, Mass.: American Academy of Arts and Sciences, 1971).

CHAPTER TEN

1. Albert Camus, *The Stranger* (New York: Alfred A. Knopf, Vintage Books, 1958), p. 154.

2. Matt. 6:33 (Revised Standard Version).

CHAPTER ELEVEN

1. Charles L. Goodell, *Followers of the Gleam* (New York: Funk & Wagnalls, 1911), chap. 3.

CHAPTER TWELVE

1. Letter to Willis M. Tate from Albert Cook Outler.